The ROYAL WAY OF THE CROSS

The ROYAL WAY OF THE CROSS

Letters and Spiritual Counsels of
**Francois de Salignac
de la Mothe-Fénelon**

Revised Edition

Edited by
Hal M. Helms

Translated by H. Sidney Lear

PARACLETE PRESS

Eighth Printing, November 1986

Copyright © 1982 by Paraclete Press
Orleans, MA 02653
Library of Congress Catalog Card Number: 80-67874
ISBN: 0-941478-00-9
All Rights Reserved
Published by Paraclete Press
Printed in the United States of America

And dost thou pretend to seek another way than this royal way, which is the way of the holy cross?

Thomas à Kempis

To Two Remarkable Women
M. Cay Andersen and M. Judy Sorensen
who
by walking the Way of the Cross
have encouraged others in it
This book is dedicated with gratitude and affection

A Commendation

I sometimes wonder, when people are confronted with a book, if they bother with a Foreword or a Preface or an Introduction. Do they say, "Oh, never mind the preliminaries and the sales-talk, let's get stuck into the book itself!"? So I have entitled this "A Commendation" in the hope that the unusual word may catch your attention!

This book will be a help to you, there is no doubt about that. But remember that any book is your servant and not your master (with the exception of the New Testament!), so if you feel like skipping the odd page — skip it, with a clear conscience. And on the other hand, if you feel like staying on a page for quite a time (even for days), stay on it. The book is in your hands to help you in your love of God, not to hang you up.

Fenelon was involved in controversy, and at one time was censured by the Holy See; but all that is over and done with, and I do not think it would be profitable to rehash it. It was just a technicality about methods of prayer; and in any case, we are nowadays much more free in our prayer than we used to be. It used to be rather a drill: now we recognize it much more as a conversation between lovers.

The extracts offered in this book are main-line spirituality which should be acceptable and helpful to any one who wants to follow our Lord Jesus Christ. There is nothing controversial in them — except the basic contradiction between the Way of the Cross and the Way of the World. And what Christian would want to escape that?

This is not a book to read and discard: it is a book to read and go back to, and go back to, and go back to. And as you do, may God lead you deeper into its truth and may He richly bless you.

+ Anselm

The Rt. Rev. Anselm Genders, C.R., M.A.
Ret. Bishop of Bermuda

Introduction

Fenelon's name has become familiar in recent years through the publication of forty of his letters under the title of *Let Go*. This present collection of letters and meditations gives us further counsel and wisdom from his insights and experience.

Francois de Salignac de la Mothe-Fénelon was born of noble parentage in the Castile de Fenelon, Perigord, France, in 1651. After his graduation from the Seminary of Saint Sulpice, he was ordained priest in 1675, and quickly rose to a position of importance and responsibility. At the age of twenty-seven, he was appointed superior of the Nouvelles Catholiques, a house of recent converts from Protestantism. It was a time of religious upheaval, and following the revoking of the Edict of Nantes, which removed from French Protestants the religious freedom they had previously enjoyed, Fenelon was given a mission among the Huguenots of Santionge, which he did with apparent success.

In 1688 Fenelon became acquainted with Madame Guyon, whose fame as a teacher of spiritual depth had spread through much of France, and who was prominent in royal circles. He was much impressed with her spirit and her teaching, especially as regarded "disinterested love," (meaning love that is stripped of self-centeredness or idolatry). From that time on, Fenelon's own teaching developed along much the same lines as hers, and he rose to her defense when she was suspected of heresy and condemned by a theological commission in 1695.

In 1689, having returned to Paris, he was appointed tutor to the young Duke of Burgundy, grandson of Louis XIV and heir apparent to the throne. The young duke was very head-strong, self-willed and undisciplined, and so profound was Fenelon's influence on him that he was accused later of having made the Duke too docile. Fenelon's novel, *Telemaque,* published in 1699, detailed his philosophy of education and his conviction that "kings and their policies are subject to moral law and that the true interests of the state cannot conflict with that law."

His success with the Duke's education and his valued work as spiritual director and counsellor of members of the royal court resulted in his appointment as Archbishop of Cambrai in Northern France in 1695.

In the meantime, the teachings of Madame Guyon and her spiritual mentor, Father La Combe, had come under increasing attack by some of the French clergy, especially by Fenelon's old teacher, J. B. Bossuet, the most outstanding preacher of his time, a man of great zeal for the Catholic faith and of considerable influence at the French court. Madame Guyon's teaching seems to have filled a void in the spiritual life of the time and many earnest souls were drawn to the deeper spiritual life of which she spoke and wrote. When she was attacked, she called for a theological conference to examine her work. The commission met at Issy, near Paris in 1695, and at its conclusion, 34 articles were drawn up condemning certain errors of the Quietist teaching. These articles were signed by Bossuet, Fenelon, and Madame Guyon herself.

Fenelon, however, was concerned lest the truth be lost in such condemnations, so the next year he published *Explication des maximes des saintes,* in which he set forth the difference between true and false spirituality, using the writings and experiences of many saints as verification. Bossuet immediately fiercely attacked the book, and in the years following waged a prolonged and bitter literary battle against Fenelon. The controversy cost Fenelon the confidence of Louis XIV, who dismissed him as tutor of his grandson and cut off contact between Fenelon and his pupil. After months of delay, at the insistence of Bossuet and the King of France, Pope Innocent XII issued a bull condemning 23 propositions in Fenelon's book. He is said to have been very reluctant to do this, and to have remarked that "Fenelon erred by loving God too much!"

Thenceforth Fenelon was banished from the royal court and exiled in his own diocese of Cambrai. He submitted completely to the judgment against his writing, and spent his remaining years tending his diocese, aiding the poor and suffering, and offering spiritual counsel to those who sought him out. Many of his letters were written during this long exile, and were so treasured that they were gathered after his death in 1715 and published.

Their unique strength and value seem due to the fact that Fenelon allowed God to bring the Cross into his own life, stripping him of honor and preferment, costing him friendships and much that would normally be considered important to human happiness. He bore it with grace, believing that God was permitting it to happen for his good. Out of this death he was able to bring light and counsel to many others who needed to understand their own lives better in the light of the Cross. The fact that succeeding generations have continued to value them is mute testimony to the spiritual principle that life comes out of death to self.

It is important to remember as one reads these letters and meditations that they were originally written to individuals, and that they often deal with very specific problems. The same is true, of course, of St. Paul's letters in the New Testament. In both cases it is necessary to bear this in mind to avoid stressing some point out of the context and spirit of the whole. For example, Fenelon speaks in one of his letters about the need for softening the corrective word to others. To whom was he speaking? To someone, no doubt, whose self-righteousness and anger made such words a weapon and expression of self. On the other hand, he rebukes someone else for oversensitivity to correction, calling such sensitivity the evidence of self-love. He himself invites correction without sparing, and certainly does not mince words or equivocate in speaking truth to those for whom he was responsible. All this needs to be borne in mind when reading or interpreting any individual passage.

This compilation seeks to set forth a multi-faceted view of the "royal way of the Cross," as Fenelon saw and expressed it. He believed that God was in all things in his own life and in the lives of his readers — in things fair and things unfair, things pleasant and things unpleasant. And he invites us to share this way of looking at life.

The translation, with minor editorial changes, is that of H. Sidney Lear, whose interest in Fenelon's work resulted in the publication of several excellent volumes in the late nineteenth century, now out of print.

Hal M. Helms

Table of Contents

Seeing Our True Spiritual State Before God

In order to make your prayer profitable, and as earnest as you desire, it would be well from the beginning to figure yourself as a poor, naked, miserable wretch, perishing of hunger, who knows but one man of whom he can ask or hope for help; or as a sick person, covered with sores and ready to die unless some pitiful physician will take him in hand and heal him. These are true pictures of our condition before God. Your soul is more bare of heavenly treasure than that poor beggar is of earthly possessions; you need them more urgently, and there is none save God of whom you can ask or expect them. Again, your soul is infinitely more sinsick than that sore-stricken patient, and God alone can heal you. Everything depends on His being moved by your prayers. He is able for all this: but remember that He wills only to do when He is asked earnestly, and with real neediness.

When once penetrated with this truth, as you ought to be in order to set-about prayer rightly, then proceed to read over the subject of your meditation, either in Holy Scripture or in whatever book you may be using. Pause after a verse or two, to follow out such reflections as God may put into your mind. And in order to help forward your beginnings, to rouse your mind from its ordinary inattention, you would do well to thank Him for His Word, the oracle by which He teaches us His will, and for His willingness to teach us; and it would be well to humble yourself and confess that you have not heeded His teaching better or profited by it more, examining wherein you have specially neglected it, or are neglecting it, and how far your life has been in conformity to God's will or in opposition to it. Lay your shame before God. Reflect on the occasions which cause you to commit these faults; the best means of avoiding or remedying them; what the Lord justly requires of you that you may keep from such falls and repent of the past. Think of how greatly you are bound to obey, however hard it may seem, how profitable it is to do so, how disgraceful and dangerous it would be to leave it undone. Remember that we are weakness itself, as daily experience proves, and offer yourself to Jesus Christ; abhor your cowardice and faithlessness; pray Him to fill your heart with all that He would see in it; ask Him to strengthen this will, so that you may go on doing better; trust in His goodness and in His solemn promises never to forsake us in time of need. Lean upon His words, and rest in the hope that He will confirm that which He has wrought in you so far.

Concerning a Real Conversion

We must yield to God when He urges us to let Him reign with us.

Did you hesitate or resist so much when the world sought to seduce you through its passions and pleasures? Did you resist evil as stoutly as you resist what is good? When it is a question of going astray, being corrupted, lost, of acting against the inmost consciousness of heart and reason by indulging vanity or sensual pleasure, we are not so afraid of "going too far"; we choose, we yield unreservedly. But when the question is to believe that we, who did not make ourselves, were made by an All-wise, All-powerful Hand—to acknowledge that we owe all to Him from Whom we received all, and Who made us for Himself; then we begin to hesitate, to deliberate, to foster subtle doubts as to the simplest, plainest matters; we are afraid of being credulous, we mistrust our own feelings, we shift our ground. We fear to give too much to Him for Whom nothing can be too much, though we never gave Him anything yet; we are actually ashamed of ceasing to be ungrateful, and of letting the world see that we want to serve Him! In a word, we are as timid, shrinking, and shy about what is good, as we were bold and unhesitatingly decided concerning what is evil.

All I would ask of you is simply now to follow the leadings of your inmost heart towards what is good, as you once followed those of your worldly passions towards evil. Whenever you examine the foundation of your religion, you will easily see that there is nothing substantial to be said against it, and that those who oppose it do so only to evade the rules of holy living, rejecting God out of self-seeking. But in all honesty, is it fair to be so broad-minded on behalf of self, and so narrow where God is concerned?

Do not argue. Either listen to your own heart, in which God, so long forgotten, is now speaking lovingly, notwithstanding past unfaithfulness; or consult such friends as you know to be right-minded and sincere. Ask them what they find God's service to be; whether they repent having pledged themselves to it, and whether they think they were too credulous or too bold in their conversion. They, like you, were in the world; ask whether they regret having forsaken it, and whether the intoxication of Babylon is sweeter than the peace of Zion? No, indeed! Whatever crosses may attend the Christian's life, he need never lose that blessed peace of heart through which one accepts every suffering, desiring no happiness which God denies. Can the world give as much? You can tell. Are men of the world always satisfied with everything that comes to them, content without all they have not? Do they do all out of love and with their heart?

What are you afraid of? Of leaving that which will soon leave you?

What are you afraid of? Of following too much goodness, finding a too-loving God; of being drawn by an attraction which is stronger than self, or the charms of this poor world?

What are you afraid of? Of becoming too humble, too detached, too pure, too true, too reasonable, too grateful to your Father which is in heaven? I pray you, be afraid of nothing so much as of this false fear—this foolish, worldly wisdom which hesitates between God and self, between vice and virtue, between gratitude and ingratitude, between life and death.

The reader should remember that these letters were originally written to individuals, and the counsel given is meant for specific situations. One should avoid taking any specific advice given as applying to one's life situation today. Instead, they should be read for the wisdom and general counsel which they so richly contain.

3

What Does He Ask of You?

G od has not forgotten you, since He stirs up so eager a desire for your salvation in me.

What does He ask of you, save to be happy? Have you not realized that one is happy in loving Him? Have you not felt that there is no other real happiness, whatever excitement may be found in sensual pleasures, apart from Him? Since, then, you know where to find the Fountain of Life, and have of old drunk thereof, why would you seek foul, earthly cisterns? Bright, happy days, lighted up by the soft rays of loving mercy, when will ye return? When will it be given me to see this child of God reclaimed by His powerful hand, filled with His favor, and the blessings of His holy feast; causing joy in heaven, despising earth, and laden with a fund of humility and zeal from his experience of human frailty and sin?

Do whatever you will, only love God, and let His love, revived in your heart be your guide. Many times I have trembled for you: put an end to my fears! Your ears are not yet closed to the sublime language of truth; your heart is made to feel its charms. "Taste and see" the pleasant bread daily spread for us at our Father's table. With such support, who can fear that anything else will be lacking?

I know what it is to be weak; I am a thousand times weaker than you. It is very profitable to have realized what one is; but do not add to that weakness, which is inseparable from our human nature, an estrangement from the very means of strength. Only hearken inwardly to Him and despise boldly that which is despicable.

4

Fear of Being Wrong

Your spiritual progress is more hindered by your excessive fear of giving way to enjoyment in ordinary, innocent things, than it ever could be by that enjoyment itself. Of course, self-indulgence is always to be avoided, especially when we need self-restraint; but you are seriously injuring yourself by keeping up a perpetual effort to resist even the smallest involuntary pleasure in the details of a well-regulated life. I would have you steadily resist such a tendency. I do not approve of your efforts to reject the enjoyment inevitably attending upon simple food and needed rest. Since you are ordered to take milk, you ought to obey your doctor. Submit without arguing; otherwise you will involve yourself endlessly and to no avail. Speak honestly about your concerns about your health to your doctor, then leave him to decide and give no heed to your own fancies. But obey quietly; that should be the aim of your courage and steadfastness. Without this

25

you will not acquire the peace which God's children possess, nor will you deserve it. Bear all annoyances of your present condition, which is full of inconveniences and discomfort, in a penitential spirit; these are the penances God assigns you, and far more useful that you may choose for yourself. There is no spot in the world where you would not find yourself beset with your natural taste for enjoyment. Even the strictest solitude would have its thorns.

The best state to be in is that in which God's hand holds you: do not look beyond it, and be content to accept His will from one moment to another in the spirit of mortification and renunciation. But this acquiescence must be full of trust in God, who loves you all the more for not sparing you. You ought to be scrupulous about your scruples rather than about your enjoyment of innocent, ordinary things.

Scruples is a term often appearing in the writings of Fenelon. It refers to an excessive concern to be right in small details, particularly where religious restrictions or denials are concerned. We would probably call it a "legalistic" attitude today. Jesus referred to the Pharisees' scruples when He spoke of washing the outside of the cup, while within was all manner of filth and uncleanness which they were overlooking. That is the kind of thing Fenelon is concerned with in those he is counseling.

5

False and Real Humility

That is false humility which believes itself unworthy of God's goodness and dares not look to it with trust. True humility lies in seeing our own unworthiness and giving ourselves up to God, never doubting that He can work out the greatest results for and in us. If God's success depends on finding our foundations already laid, we might well fear that our sins had destroyed our chances. But God needs nothing that is in us. He can never find anything there except what He Himself has given us. No, we may go further and say that the absolute nothingness of the creature, bound up as it is with sin in a faithless soul, is the fittest of all subjects for the reception of His grace. He delights to pour it out on such, for these sinful souls which have never experienced anything but their own weakness cannot claim any of God's gifts as their own possession. It is thus as St. Paul says, "God has chosen the foolish things of the world to confound the wise."

Do not fear then, that your past faithlessness need make you unworthy of God's mercy. Nothing is so worthy of mercy as utter weakness. He came from heaven to earth to seek sinners, not just men; to seek that which was lost—as indeed all were lost but for Him. The physician seeks the sick, not the healthy. Oh, how God loves those who come boldly to Him in their foul, ragged garments, and ask, as of a father, for some garment worthy of Him!

You wait to be familiar till God shows a smiling face; but I tell you that if you will open your heart thoroughly to Him, you will cease to trouble about the aspect of His face. Let Him turn a severe and displeased countenance upon you as much as He will, He never loves you more than when He threatens, for He threatens only to prove, to humble, to detach souls. Do you want the consolation God can give, or do you want God Himself? If it is the first, then you do not love God for His own sake, but for yours; and in this case you deserve nothing from Him. But if you seek Him simply, you will find Him even more truly when He tries you than when He comforts you. When He comforts you, you have cause to fear, lest you care more for His gifts than for Himself; but when He deals roughly with you and you hold on fast, it is to Him alone that you cling. The real time for progress is not when we delight in a conscious sweetness, but when faith is dry and cold — if we do not yield to discouragement.

Leave it all to God; it is not your business to judge how He should deal with you, because He knows far better than you what is good for you. You deserve a certain amount of trial and dryness. Bear it patiently! God does His part when He repulses you. Try to do yours too, and that is to love Him without waiting for Him to assure you of His love for you. Your love is a guarantee of His; your confidence will disarm Him, and turn all His severity into tenderness. Even if He were not to grow tender, you ought to give yourself up to His just dealings, and accept His intention of nailing you to the Cross in union with His beloved Son, Jesus.

Such, my friend, is the solid food of pure faith and generous love with which you should sustain your soul. I pray that God may make you strong under your troubles.

Expect all, and all will be given you. God and IIis peace will be with you!

The Deceitfulness of Self-Love

Generally speaking, I should fear that reading about extraordinary spiritual matters tends to affect weak imaginations to excess. Moreover, self-love easily flatters itself that it has attained the altitudes which it has admired in books. It seems to me that the only course in such a case is to take no notice of such things. I advise you never to dwell voluntarily on "extraordinary experiences." This is the real way of discovering how much self-conceit has to do with these supposed gifts. Nothing tends so much to pique self-conceit and bring illusions to light, as a simple direction to set aside the marvelous, and to require a person who aspires to the marvelous to act as though nothing of the sort existed. Without such a test, I do not think a person can be proved thoroughly, and without it, I do not think due caution has been taken against delusion.

The Blessed John of the Cross advises souls to look beyond such light, and to abide in the twilight of simple faith. If the gifts are real, such detachment will not hinder them from leaving their marks upon the soul; if not, such uncompromising faith will be a sure guarantee against delusion. Moreover, such a line will not keep a soul back from God's true leadings, for there is no opposition. It can only vex self-conceit, which finds a hidden complacency in such unusual gifts; and that self-conceit is the very thing which needs pruning. Or even if such gifts are unquestionably real and good, it is most important to learn detachment from them, and live by simple faith. However excellent the gifts may be, detachment from them is better still. "And yet show I you a more excellent way"— the way of faith and love; not clinging either to sight, feeling, or taste—only to obedience to the Beloved One. Such a way is simple, real, straightforward, free from the snares of pride.

On Criticizing Others

It seems to me that you need greater liberality as to the faults of others. I grant you that you cannot help seeing them when they are forced upon you, or avoid your inevitable conclusions as to the principles on which some seem to act. Neither can you avert a certain annoyance which such things cause. Suffice it if you try to bear with obvious faults, avoiding judging such as are doubtful, and resist the dislike which estranges you from people.

Perfection finds it easy to bear with the imperfections of others, and to be all things to all men. One ought to learn to put up with the most obvious faults in worthy souls, and to leave them alone until God gives the sign for a gradual weeding; else one is likely to tear up the good grain with the weeds. God often leaves certain infirmities besetting the most advanced souls, such as seem quite out of character with their excellence;

just as in reclaimed ground men leave tokens to show how extensive the work of clearance has been. God leaves such tokens to show whence He has brought them.

All such must labor in their own measure at self-amendment, and you must labor to endure their imperfections. Your own experience will teach you that correction is a bitter thing; and as you know this, give heed to soften it to others.[1] It is not your great zeal to correct others for their own sake as much as it is your perfectionism which shuts your heart to them.

I entreat you more than ever not to spare any of my faults. Even should you think you detect such as do not really exist, it will not be a great misfortune. If your admonitions wound me, it will show you have touched a tender place, and so you will do me service in exercising my humility, and accustoming me to bear reproof. I need humiliation more than most men, by reason of my naturally proud character, and because God requires a more absolute death to all pride of me. I greatly need this honesty, and I trust that so far from disuniting us, it will draw us closer together.

[1]See my discussion in the Introduction. *Ed.*

False Notions
of Spiritual Progress

Almost all who aim at serving God do so more or less
for their own sake. They want to win, not to lose; to
be comforted, not to suffer; to possess, not to be despoiled;
to increase, not to diminish. Yet all the while our whole
interior progress consists in losing, sacrificing, decreasing,
humbling, and stripping self even of God's own gifts, so as to
be more wholly His. We are often like an invalid who feels his
pulse fifty times in the day, and wants the doctor to be perpetually ordering some fresh treatment, or telling him how much
better he is.

This is very much all the use that some people make of their
spiritual director or pastor. They move round and round in a
petty circle of easy virtues, never stepping beyond it heartily
and generously; while the director (like the physician) is

expected to soothe, comfort, encourage, foster delicacy and perfectionism, only ordering little sedative treatments, which drop into mere habit and routine. As soon as they are deprived of sensible grace, which is as the milk of babes, such people fancy that all is lost. But this is a plain proof that they cling overmuch to means, overlooking the end, and that self is their main object.

Privations are the food of strong minds: they invigorate the soul, take it out of itself, and offer it as a living sacrifice to God. But weak people are in despair at the first touch of privation. They fancy that all their work is being overthrown just when it is really beginning to be solidly fixed and thoroughly purified. They are willing to let God do what He will with them, *provided always* it be something great and perfect; but they have no notion of being cast down and crushed, or of being offered as a sacrifice to be consumed by the Divine flames. They seek to live by pure faith, yet want to retain all their worldly wisdom, to be as children, yet great in their own eyes. But what a spiritual mirage this is!

On the Right Use of Trials

People find it very hard to believe that God heaps crosses on those He loves out of lovingkindness. "Why should He take pleasure in causing us to suffer?" they ask. Could He not make us good without making us so miserable?" Yes, doubtless God could do so, for to Him all things are possible. His all-powerful hands hold the hearts of men and turn them as He pleases, as he who commands the source of a reservoir turns the stream whither he will. But though God could save us without crosses, He has not willed to do so, just as He has willed that men should grow up through the weakness and troubles of childhood, instead of being born fully developed men. He is the Master; we can only be silent and adore His infinite wisdom without understanding it. The one thing we do see plainly is that we cannot become really good save in so far as we become humble, unselfish, in all things turning from self to God.

But as that grace operates, it cannot (save through a miracle of the same grace) be other than painful, and God does not perform continual miracles in the order of grace any more than in the order of nature. It would be as great a miracle to see one full of himself die suddenly to self-consciousness and self-interest as it would be to see a child go to bed a mere child and rise up the next morning a man of thirty! God hides His work beneath a series of imperceptible events, both in grace and nature, and thus He subjects us to the mysteries of faith. Not only does He accomplish His work gradually, but He does it by the most simple and likely means, so that its success appears natural to men. Otherwise all that God does would be as a perpetual miracle, which would overthrow the life of faith by which He would have us exist.

Such a life of faith is necessary, not only to mold the good, by causing us to sacrifice our own reason amid a world of darkness, but also to blind those whose presumption misleads them. Such men behold God's works without comprehending them, and take them to be simply natural. They are without true understanding, since that is only given to those who mistrust their own judgment and the proud wisdom of man.

So it is to insure that the operation of grace may remain a mystery of faith that God permits it to be slow and painful. He makes use of the inconstancy, the ingratitude of men, the disappointments, the failures which attend human prosperity, to detach us from the creature and its good things. He opens our eyes by letting us realize our own weakness and evil in countless falls. It all seems to go on in the natural course of events, and this series of apparently natural causes consumes us like a slow fire. We would much rather be consumed at once by the flames of pure love, but so speedy a process would cost us nothing. It is utter selfishness that we desire to attain perfection so cheaply and so fast.

On Prolonged Trials

Why do we rebel against our prolonged trials? Because of self-love; and it is that very self-love that God purposes to destroy, for so long as we cleave to self, His work is not achieved.

What right have we to complain? We suffer from an excessive attachment to the creature — above all to self. God orders a series of events which detach us gradually from the creature first, and finally from the self also. The operation is painful, but our corruption makes it needful, and therefore it is we who suffer so keenly. If the flesh were sound, the surgeon would not need to probe it; he uses the knife in proportion to the depth of the wound and the extent of proud flesh. If we feel his operation too keenly, it is because the disease is active. Is it cruelty which makes the surgeon probe us to the quick? No, far otherwise — it is skill and kindness; he would do the same by his only child.

Even so God treats us. He never willingly puts us to any pain. His fatherly heart does not desire to grieve us, but He cuts to the quick that He may heal the ulcers of our spiritual being. He must tear from us that which we love wrongly, unreasonably, or excessively, that which hinders His love. And in so doing, He causes us to cry out like a child from whom one takes the knife with which it would maim or kill itself. We cry loudly in our despair, and murmur against God, as the petulant babe against its mother; but He lets us cry, and saves us nevertheless! He only afflicts us for our correction; even when He seems to overwhelm us, it is for our own good, and to spare us the greater evil we would do to ourselves. The things for which we weep would have caused us eternal woe. That which we count as loss was then indeed most lost when we fancied it our own. God has stored it up safely, to be returned to us in eternity, which is fast drawing near. He only deprives us of the things we prize in order to teach us to love them purely, truly, and highly; in order that we may enjoy them forever in His presence; in order to do a hundred-fold better for us than we can even desire for ourselves.

Nothing can happen in the world but by God's permissive will.[1] He does all, arranges all, makes all to be as it is. He counts the hairs of our head, the leaves of every tree, the sand on the seashore, the drops of water from the mighty ocean. When He made the world, His wisdom weighed and measured every atom. Every moment He renews and sustains the breath of life. He knows the number of our days; He holds the cords of life or death. What seems to us weightiest is as nothing in the eyes of God; a little longer or shorter life becomes an imperceptible difference before Him. What matters whether this frail vessel, this poor clay, be thrown aside a little sooner or later? How short-sighted and erring we are! We are aghast at the death of one in the flower of his age. "What a sad loss!" men cry out. But to whom is the loss? What does he who dies lose? Some few years of vanity, delusion, and peril! God takes him away from the evil, and saves him from his own weakness and the world's wickedness. What do they lose who love him? The danger of earthly happiness, a treacherous delight, a snare which caused them to forget God and their own welfare; but in truth they gain the blessing of detachment through the cross. That same blow by which he who dies is saved fits those who are left to work out their salvation in hope. Surely, then, it is true that God is very good, very loving, very pitiful to our real needs, even when He seems to overwhelm us, and we are most tempted to call Him hard!

It is owing to the sensitiveness of self-love that we are so alive to our own condition. The sick man who cannot sleep thinks the night is endless, yet it is no longer than any other night. In our cowardice, we exaggerate all we suffer; our pain may be severe, but we make it worse by shrinking under it. The real way to get relief is to give one's self up heartily to God; to accept suffering because God sends it to purify us and make us worthier of Him. The world smiled upon you, and was as a poison to your soul. Would you wish to go on in ease, pleasure, display, in the pride of life, and soul-destroying luxury, clinging to the world, which is Christ's enemy, rejecting the cross, which alone can sanctify you—up to the hour of death? The world will turn away, forget, despise, ignore you. Well, need you wonder that the world is worldly, unjust, deceitful, treacherous? Yet you are not ashamed to love this world, from which God snatches you to deliver you from its bondage and make you free, and you complain of your very deliverance. You are your own enemy when you are so alive to the world's indifference, and when you cannot endure what is for your real good, and when you so keenly regret the loss of what is fatal to you. This is the source of all your grief and pain.

[1] I have taken the liberty of adding "permissive" to avoid any temptation to call God the author of evil. *Ed.*

41

11

On Anxiety About the Future

The future is in God's hands, not yours. God will rule it according to your need. But if you seek to forecast it in your own wisdom, you will gain nothing but anxiety and anticipation of inevitable trouble. Try only to make use of each day; each day brings its own good and evil, and sometimes what seems evil becomes good if we leave it to God, and do not forestall Him with our impatience.

Be sure that God will grant you whatever time you need to attain to Him. Perhaps He may not give you as much as you would like for your own plans, or to please yourself under the pretext of seeking spiritual perfection, but you will find that neither time nor opportunity for renunciation of self and self-pleasing will be lacking. All other time is lost, however well spent it may seem. Be assured that you will find all such matters adapted to your real needs. In proportion as God upsets your own inclinations He will uphold your weakness. Do not be afraid; leave all to Him. Only by a quiet, pleasant, well-regulated system of occupation, avert melancholy and depression, which are the most dangerous temptations to your natural disposition.

You will always find freedom in God so long as you do not give way to the false idea that you have lost your freedom.

12

On the Struggle of Self-Will

Your troubles come from jealousy, or the sensitive self-love, or from some deep-down scruple which is closely allied to self-love. And such troubles always carry disturbance with them. Both cause and effect prove that they are real temptations.

The Spirit of God never inspires us with self-conceit; and so far from creating disturbance, He always fills the heart with peace. What could be more certain proof of temptation than to see you in a kind of despair, rebelling against everything which God gives you to lead you to Himself? Such rebellion is not natural, but God allows temptation to drive you to such an extremity in order that you may more easily recognize that it *is* temptation.

In the same way, He allows you to fall into certain faults in the presence of others, which are altogether contrary to your excessive delicacy and discretion, in order to mortify that delicacy and discretion which you cherish so jealously. He causes the ground under you to give way, in order that you may not find any conscious support, either in yourself or in anyone else. Further, He allows you to fancy that your neighbor judges you quite other than he really does, in order that your self-conceit may lose any flattering prop in that direction.

The remedy is severe, but it needed nothing less to free you from yourself, and to storm the battlements of your pride. You want to die, but to die without any pain and in full health! You want to be tried, but only while looking on with conscious superiority to the trial. It is a saying of the old lawyers with respect to donations: you cannot give and hold. You must give all or nothing when God asks it. If you have not courage to give, at least let Him take.

13

On Self-Deceit

Nothing so feeds self-conceit as believing that you are wholly devoted to others, and never self-seeking, believing that one is quite free from self-love and always generously devoted to one's neighbors.

But all this devotion which seems to be for others is really for yourself. Your self-love reaches the point of perpetual self-congratulation in the mistaken belief that you are free from self-love itself. All your anxiety is fear that you might not be fully satisfied with yourself, and this is the root of your scruples.

If you thought of nothing but God and His glory, you would be as keen and sensitive to the losses of others as to your own. But it is the "I" which makes you so keen and sensitive. You want God as well as man to be always satisfied with you, and you want to be satisfied with *yourself* in all your dealings with God.

You are not used to being content with a simple good-will. Your self-love wants a lively feeling, a reassuring pleasure, some kind of charm or excitement. You are too much guided by imagination, and suppose that your mind and will are inactive unless you are conscious of their workings. Thus you depend on a kind of excitement similar to that which the passions or the theatre arouse.

Because of your excessive refinement, you fall into the opposite extreme — a real coarseness of imagination. Nothing is more opposed to the life of faith and to true wisdom.

There is no more dangerous opening to delusion than the false ways by which people try to avoid delusion. It is imagination which leads us astray; and the certainty which we seek through imagination, feeling and taste, is one of the most dangerous sources from which fanaticism springs.

This is the gulf of vanity and corruption which God would have you discover in your own heart: you must look on it with the calm and simplicity which belong to true humility. It is self-love which makes us so inconsolable at seeing one's own imperfections. To stand face to face with them, however, not flattering or tolerating them, seeking to correct one's self without becoming pettish — this is to desire what is good for its own sake, and for God's sake, rather than merely treating it as a self-satisfying decoration.

So do turn your concern against this useless search of yours after the *self*-satisfaction you find in doing right.

Should you be so sensitive, even if others formed an unjust opinion of you? Many holy souls have submitted to being condemned unjustly by prejudiced people. Mistrust your imagination and your intellect!

I shall pray continually for you.

48

14

On the Dangers of Imagination

I think you ought to abstain wholly from your imaginary dialogues. Although some may tend to kindly pious feelings, I think it is a dangerous habit for you. From such as these you will unconsciously pass on to others, which will foster your excitement, or encourage your love of the world. Far better to suppress them all. I do not mean that you should stop them forcibly — you might as well try to stop a torrent; enough if you do not voluntarily harbor them. When you perceive that your imagination is beginning to work, be satisfied with turning to God, without directly combating these fancies. Let them drop, occupying yourself in some useful way. If it be a time of meditation or prayer, such idle thoughts should be treated as distractions. Return, then, quietly to God as soon as you are conscious of them, but do so without anxiety, scruples, or agitation. If, on the other hand, such imaginations trouble you when engaged in external work, the work will help you to resist such castle building. It would even be well at first to find some companion, or to set about some difficult task, with a view to breaking the thread of such thoughts and getting rid of the habit.

You must positively suppress this trifling of the imagination. It is a pure waste of time, a very dangerous occupation, and a temptation voluntarily incurred. It is a duty never to yield to it voluntarily. Perhaps, owing to habit, your imagination will still beset you with fancies in spite of yourself; but at all events do not yield to them, and try quietly to get rid of them when you become aware that they are occupying you.

15

On the Dangers of Human Praise

I rejoice in your present tranquility. I am, however, somewhat fearful lest your self-love may too keenly relish this
ease, so different from the discomfort you have experienced.
Contrition and other humiliating circumstances are far more
profitable than success. You know that your troubles made
you find out what you never knew before about yourself; and
I am afraid lest the authority, the success and admiration which
are easily acquired among the people around you, should foster
your imperious temper, and make you self-satisfied as you
were before. Such self-satisfaction will mar the best ordered
life, because it is incompatible with humility.

We can only be humble so long as we give heed to all our
own infirmities. The consciousness of these should be pre-
dominant; the soul should feel burdened by them, groan under

them, and that groaning should be as a perpetual prayer to be set free from "the bondage of corruption," and admitted into the "glorious liberty of the children of God"; overwhelmed by its own faults, the soul should feel it deserves no deliverance from the great mercy of Jesus Christ. Woe to the soul which is self-satisfied, which treats God's gifts as its own merits, and forgets what is due to Him!

Your remedy for dissipation and dryness will be to set apart regular seasons for reading and prayer; only to mix yourself up in outward matters when it is really necessary; and to attend more to softening the harshness of your judgment, to restraining your temper, and humbling your mind, than to upholding your opinion even when it is right; and finally to humble yourself, whenever you find that an undue interest in the affairs of others has led you to forget the one all-important matter of yourself: Eternity.

"Learn of me," Jesus says to you, "for I am meek and lowly of heart and ye shall find rest unto your souls." (St. Matt. 11:29) Be sure that grace, inward peace, and the blessing of the Holy Spirit will be with you if you will maintain a gentle humility amid all your external perplexities.

16

On Dealing Wisely with the Faults of Others

Imperfect as we ourselves are, we only know ourselves partly; and the same self-love which causes our failings hides them very subtly, both from others and from ourselves.

Self-love cannot bear to see itself; the sight would overwhelm it with shame and vexation, and if it catches an accidental glimpse, it seeks some false light which may soften and condone what is so hideous. Thus we always keep up some illusion so long as we retain any self-love. To see ourselves perfectly, self-love must be rooted up, and the love of God reign solely in us, and then the same light which shows our faults would remove them. Till then we only half know ourselves, because we are only half given to God, cleaving to self a great deal more than we think, or dare to own to ourselves. When we "receive all truth," we shall see clearly; and loving ourselves only with the love of charity, we shall see ourselves as we see our neigh-

bor, without self-interest, and without flattery. Meanwhile
God spares our weakness, only showing us our true hideous-
ness in proportion to the courage He gives us to bear the sight.
He shows us first one bit, and then another, as He gradually
leads us on to amendment. Without this merciful preparation
of light and strength in due proportion, the sight of our frailty
would only tend to despair.

Those to whom spiritual guidance is entrusted should only
lay bare men's faults as God prepares the heart to see them.
One must learn to watch a fault patiently, and take no external
measure until God begins to make it felt by the inward conscience. Nay, more: one must imitate God's own way of
dealing with the soul, softening His rebuke, so that the person
rebuffed feels as if it was rather self-reproach, and a sense of
wounded love, than God rebuking. All other methods of
guidance, reproving impatiently, or because one is vexed at
infirmities, smack of earthly judgments, not the correction
of grace. It is imperfection rebuking the imperfect: it is a
subtle, clinging self-love, which cannot see anything to forgive
in the self-love of others. The greater our own self-love, the
more severe critics we shall be. Nothing is so offensive to a
haughty, sensitive, self-conceit as the self-conceit of others.
But, on the contrary, the love of God is full of consideration,
forbearance, condescension, and tenderness. It adapts itself,
waits, and never moves more than one step at a time. The less
self-love we have, the more we know how to adapt ourselves to
curing our neighbor's failings of that kind; we learn better
never to lance without putting plenty of healing ointment to the
wound, never to purge the patient without feeding him up,
never to risk an operation save when nature indicates its safety.
One learns to wait years before giving a salutary warning;
to wait till Providence prepares suitable external circumstances,
and grace opens the heart. If you persist in gathering fruit

before it is ripe, you simply waste your labor.

You say rightly that your moods keep changing, and you do not know what to say of yourself. As most of our moods are passing and complicated, our explanations are apt to become untrue before we finish making them. Something quite different takes over, and that in its turn seems unreal. So it is best to be content to say that about one's self which seems to be true at the moment one is opening one's heart. It is not necessary to tell everything methodically; suffice it to keep back nothing intentionally, and to soften nothing with the flattering touches of self-conceit. God supplies what is lacking to an upright heart according to its needs; and those (spiritual guides) who are enlightened by grace easily perceive what people do not know how to tell when the penitent is honest, simple, and unreserved.

Since our friends, too, are imperfect, they can only know us imperfectly. They often judge only from the external failings which make themselves felt in company, and which jar upon their own self-conceit. Self-conceit is a very sharp, harsh, unforgiving critic, and the same self-conceit which softens their view of their own faults makes them magnify ours. Their point of view being wholly different from ours, they see that which we do not perceive in ourselves, and overlook much that we see. They are quick to discern many things which wound their sensitive, jealous self-love, and which ours equally conceals; but they do not see those secret faults which stain our virtues more, though they offend only God. And so their maturest judgment is very superficial. My conclusion is that it is best to hearken to God in a profound inward silence, and in all simplicity to say for or against oneself whatever His light discloses to one at the moment one is seeking to open one's heart.

17

On the Danger of Self-Chosen Plans

You have withered your heart by so eagerly pressing your own wishes regardless of God's will. This is the cause of all you are suffering. You have spent a great deal of time in making plans which were mere cobwebs, and a breath of wind has blown them away. You withdrew gradually from God, and He has withdrawn from you. You must return to Him, and give yourself up unreservedly to Him: there is no other way by which you can regain peace.

Let go all your plans; God will do as He pleases with them. Even if they were to succeed through earthly means, He would not bless them. But if you offer them unreservedly to Him, He will turn everything to His own merciful purposes, whether He does what you wish or not.

The important thing is to resume prayer and communion with God, whatever dryness, distraction, or weariness you may find in it. You deserve to be rejected of God after having rejected Him for the creature so long — your patience will win Him again.

But meanwhile, persevere in your communions to strengthen your weakness. The weak need to be fed above all with Bread. Do not argue, or give heed to your fancies, but receive communion as soon as you can.

18

On Using Eager Aspirations

It is not to be wondered at that you should have a sort of jealous eagerness and ambition to advance in the spiritual life, and to be in the confidence of noteworthy servants of God.

Self-love naturally seeks successes of this kind, which are flattering to it. But the real thing that matters is, not to satisfy your ambition by some brilliant advance in virtue, or by being taken into the confidence of distinguished persons, but to mortify the flattering tendencies of self-love, to humble yourself, to love obscurity and contempt, and to seek God only.

People cannot become perfect by hearing or reading about perfection. The chief thing is not to listen to yourself, but silently to give ear to God; to renounce all vanity, and apply yourself to real virtue.

Talk little, and do much, without caring to be seen. God will teach you more than all the most experienced persons or the most spiritual books can do. What is it you want so much to know? What do you need to learn, save to be poor in spirit and to find all wisdom in Christ crucified? "Knowledge puffeth up"; it is only "charity which edifieth." (I Cor. 8:1) Do be content to aim at charity. Do you need any such great knowledge in order to love God and deny yourself for His love? You already know a great deal more than you practice. You do not need the acquirement of fresh knowledge half so much as to put in practice that which you already possess.

How people delude themselves, when they expect to advance by means of argument and inquisitiveness! Be lowly, and never expect to find in man those things which are God's only.

19

On the Need of Calming Natural Activity

I am afraid lest your natural activity should consume you amid the irksome details with which you are surrounded. You cannot take too many pains to subdue your natural temperament by prayer, and by a frequent renewal of God's Presence through the day. A Christian who grows eager over worldly trifles, and who suddenly awakes to the sense of God's Presence amid such eagerness, is like a child whose mother catches him suddenly having lost his temper over a game; he is quite ashamed at being found out.

Be it ours to abide tranquilly, fulfilling all outward duties as well as we can, while inwardly we are absorbed by Him who is alone worthy of all our love. Whenever you become conscious of the impulses of your nature, throw them aside, so that grace may possess you wholly. It is well to stop immediately when we find nature getting the upper hand. Such fidelity to grace is almost as beneficial to the body as to the soul, — there is no neglect, and yet none of Martha's trouble.[1]

[1]Referring to Luke 10:41,42. "But the Lord answered her, 'Martha, Martha, you are anxious and troubled about many things; one thing is needful. Mary has chosen the good portion, which shall not be taken from her.' "

20

On Doing All for God

What I most desire for you is a certain calmness which recollection, detachment, and love of God alone can give. St. Augustine says that whatever we love outside God, so much the less do we love Him. It is as a brook whence part of the waters is turned aside. Such a diversion takes away from that which is God's and thence arise harassment and trouble. God would have all, and His jealousy cannot endure a divided heart. The slightest affection apart from Him becomes a hindrance, and causes estrangement. The soul can only look to find peace in love without reserve.

Dissipation (a scattering abroad), the great foe of recollection, excites all human feelings, distracts the soul, and drives it from its true resting place. Further still, it kindles the senses and the imagination, and to quiet them again is a hard task, while the very effort to do so is in itself inevitably a distraction.

Concern yourself as little as possible with external matters. Give a quiet, calm attention to those things assigned to your care by Providence at proper seasons, and be sure that you can accomplish a great deal more by quiet, thoughtful work done as in God's sight, than by all the busy eagerness and over-activity of your restless nature.

21

On Trouble in the Home

It seems to me that the chief thing for you is never to despair of God's goodness, and only to mistrust yourself. The more we mistrust ourselves, and look to God only for the correction of our faults, the more it will be achieved, but it will not do to count on God without working hard one's self. Grace only works effectually in us when we, on our side, work heartily, too. You must watch, be strict with yourself, shun self-deceit, receive the most humiliating rebukes patiently, and only count yourself to be dealing faithfully with God when you are making daily practical sacrifices and self-denials.

As you think that you have said things to your husband tending to set him against his mother, you must endeavor to put this right; but do it quietly and gradually. It is very important that her son should not be in anywise estranged from such a good mother, who loves him dearly, and is so devoted to his real interests. She may from time to time do too much or too little, as easily happens to the wisest and best-intentioned people; but take it all in all, you seldom find anyone truly religious and right-minded in all respects. She may sometimes be a little quick with you concerning what she considers your real good; but she loves you, — that I can say from my own knowledge, — and what you feel to be excessive is but an excess of affection. Indeed, you ought to strive diligently to draw the mother and son together, both for his sake and for your own; but try to do it without vexing and exciting yourself.

If you have committed some serious faults in this matter, you must bear your inward humiliation without being disheartened. Try henceforward to avoid anything which could tend to the repetition of such errors, and be careful to neglect no opportunity of repairing the past.

I have noticed one excellent point in you, and that is: your openness with your mother-in-law. Keep this up, — tell her everything, whatever it may cost you; you know by experience how she will receive it, and God's blessing will be on such straightforward simplicity. You see how good He is to you, little as you have responded to His correction. Would you misuse His patience, and turn it against Himself, by treating His mercies with contempt?

How glad I shall be if I can hear that God has opened your heart, and taught you to mistrust your imagination; and that you have learned to cast aside your indolence, and go to work steadily at all your duties. Then you would find as much freedom and peace as now you have anxiety, depression and uncertainty.

You see by the freedom with which I speak how sincerely I am devoted to you.

(This meditation was written to a young woman living with her mother-in-law. Fenelon had known and counselled her from childhood.)

22

On the Life of Peace

Go on amid the shadows in evangelic simplicity, not stopping short either in feelings, or tastes, or the light of reason, or any extraordinary gifts. Be content to believe, to obey, to die unto self, according to that state of life in which God has placed you.

You must not be discouraged by your involuntary distractions, which arise from your lively imagination and your active habits in business. Enough if you do not encourage such distractions in times of prayer by yielding too easily to a voluntary dissipation (a scattering abroad) of mind all through the day.

People pour themselves out too much. They perform even good works with too much eagerness and excitement; they indulge their tastes and fancies, and then God punishes all this in their times of prayer. You must learn to act calmly and in continual dependence on the Spirit of grace, which means mortification of all the hidden works of self-love.

Habitual intention, which is a reaching forth of the inmost soul to God, will suffice. This is to live in the presence of God. Passing events would not find you thus minded, were it otherwise. Be still, and do not forfeit what you have at home by turning to seek abroad what you will not find. Never neglect out of mere carelessness to try and make your intentions more definite, but meanwhile your undefined, undeveloped intentions are good.

A peaceful heart is a good sign, provided further that you heartily and lovingly obey God, and are watchful against self-love.

Make use of your imperfections to learn self-detachment, and cleave to God only. Try to grow in all goodness, not that you may find a dangerous self-satisfaction therein, but that you may do the will of your Beloved.

Try to be simple, putting aside anxious looking backward, which self-love encourages under various pretexts. It will only disturb you and prove a snare. Those who lead a recollected, mortified, dependent life, through real desire to love God, will be quickly warned by that love whenever they sin against it; and as soon as you feel such warnings, pause. I repeat my injunction: be at rest.

May God keep you in His own unity and in the grace of His Holy Spirit.

23

To One in Spiritual Distress

You see by God's light in the depth of your conscience what grace requires of you, but you are resisting God, and hence comes your trouble.

You start by saying, "It is impossible that I can do what is required of me." But this is a temptation of despair. Despair of yourself as much as you please, but not of God. He is both loving and powerful, and He will deal with you according to the measure of your faith. If you believe all, you will attain all — you will move mountains; but if you believe nothing, you will receive nothing, only it will be your own fault. Remember Abraham, who hoped against hope; and imitate the Blessed Virgin, who, when what seemed wholly impossible was set before her, answered unhesitatingly, "Be it unto me according to Thy Word."

So do not shut up your heart. It is not merely that you cannot do what is required of you, so restricted is your heart; but yet more you do not want to be able to do it. You do not wish to have your heart enlarged. You are afraid lest it should be done. How can you expect grace to win entrance into a heart so resolutely closed against it? All that I would ask of you is to acquiesce calmly and in a spirit of faith, and not give ear to your own suggestions. Provided you will yield meekly and gradually regain peace through recollection, everything will be achieved by degrees, and what in your present state of temptation seems impossible will become easy. Then we shall have you saying, ''What, is this all?''

Why so much despair and outcry for so simple a matter which God is bringing about and preparing so lovingly? Have a care, lest in resisting Him you should estrange yourself from Him. All your religion would prove hollow if you should fail in this essential point — all would lapse into mere indulgence of tastes and tendencies. May God not allow you to fall away! There is more danger in the risk of resisting God than in the heaviest of other sorrows. Crosses borne with quiet endurance, lowliness, simplicity, and abnegation of self, unite us to Jesus Christ crucified, and work untold good; but crosses which we reject through self-estimation and self-will separate us from Him, contract the heart, and by degrees dry up the fountain of grace. Yield humbly, therefore, without trusting to yourself, mere broken reed that you are, and say, ''To Him nothing is impossible.'' He only asks one ''Yes,'' spoken in pure faith.

24

On Bearing the Bad Opinions of the World

The world, always too ready to think evil of good people, assumes that there are none such on the earth. Some rejoice to think so, and triumph maliciously; others are troubled, and in spite of a certain desire for what is good, they hold aloof from piety out of mistrust of the pious.

People are astonished to see a man who has seemed to be religious, or who, more correctly speaking, has been really converted while living in solitude, relapse into old ways and habits when he is confronted once more with the world. Did they not know before that men are frail, that the world is full of contagion, and that weak human beings can only stand upright by shunning occasions of falling? What new thing has happened? Surely this is a great fuss about the fall of a rootless tree, on which every wind blew! After all, are there not hypocrits in honesty as well as in religion to be found in the world? And ought we to conclude that there are no honest people because we find some false? When the world triumphs over a scandal (of one falling) it shows how little it knows about mankind or about virtue.

We may well be grieved at such a scandal, but those who know the depths of human frailty, and how even the little good we do is but a borrowed thing, will be surprised at nothing. Let him who stands upright tremble lest he fall; let him who is prostrate, wallowing in the mire, not triumph because he sees one fall who seemed able to stand alone.

Our confidence is neither in frail men nor in ourselves, as frail as others. Our confidence is in God only, the one unchanging Truth. Let all mankind prove themselves to be mere men — that is to say, nought save falsehood and sin. Let them be carried away by the torrent of iniquity. Still God's truth will not be weakened, and the world will but show itself as more hateful than ever in having corrupted those who were seeking after virtue.

As to hypocrites, time always unmasks them, and they are sure to expose themselves one way or another. They are hypocrites only with the object of enjoying the fruits of their hypocrisy. Either their life is sensual and pleasure-seeking, or their conduct self-interested and ambitious. One sees them cajoling, flattering, playing all manner of parts, whereas real virtue is simple, single-minded, free from impressive airs or mystery. It does not rise and fall, it is never jealous of the success or reputation of others. It does the smallest amount of wrong that it can, lets itself be criticized in silence, is content with small things, is free from cabals, maneuverings, and pretensions. Take it or leave it, it is always the same. Hypocrisy may imitate all this, but very roughly. If it deceives anyone, it will only be through their lack of discernment or of experience in real virtue. People who do not understand diamonds, or who do not examine them closely, may take false stones to be real. But all the same there are such things as real diamonds, and it is not impossible to distinguish them.

One thing is true. In order to trust fair-seeming people, we should be able to recognize their conduct as simple, steadfast, solid, and well tried under difficulty, free from affectation, while firm and vigorous in all that is essential.

25

On Christian Perfection

Christian perfection is not the strict, wearisome constrained thing many suppose it to be. It requires a person to give himself to God with his whole heart, and so soon as this is accomplished, whatever he is called upon to do for God becomes easy. Those who are wholly God's are always satisfied, for they desire only that which He wills, and are ready to do whatever He requires. They are ready to strip themselves of all things, and are sure to find a hundredfold in that nakedness. This hundredfold happiness which the true children of God possess amid all the troubles of this world consists in a peaceful conscience, freedom of spirit, a welcome resignation of all things to God, the joyful sense of His light ever growing stronger within their heart, and a thorough deliverance from all tyrannous fears and longings after worldly things. They make sacrifices, but for Him they love best. They suffer, but willingly, and realizing such suffering to be better than any worldly joy; their body may be diseased, their mind weak and shrinking, but their will is firm and steadfast, and they can say a hearty *Amen* to every blow which it pleases God to deal them.

What God requires is an undivided will — a yielding will, desiring only what He desires, rejecting only what He rejects, and both unreservedly. Where such a mind is, everything turns to good, and its very amusements become good works. Happy indeed is such an one! He is delivered from all his own passions, — from the judgments of men, their unkindness, their slavish maxims, their cold, heartless mockery; from the troubles of what the world calls fortune; from the treachery or forgetfulness of friends, the snares of enemies, his own weakness; from the weariness of this brief life, the terrors of an unholy death, the bitter remorse which follows sin, and from the eternal condemnation of God. From all these endless evils the Christian is set free. He has resigned his will to God and knows no will save His, and thus faith and hope are his comfort amid all possible sorrows.

Is it not a grievous mistake to be afraid to give yourself to God and to commit yourself to so blessed a state of things? Blessed are they who throw themselves headlong and blindfold into the arms of "the Father of all mercies and the God of all comfort." (2 Cor. 1:3) Nothing remains for them except to know Him better and better. Their only fear is that they may not be quick enough to see what He requires. Directly upon discovering any fresh light from His Law, they "rejoice as one that findeth a hid treasure." Let what may befall the true Christian, all is well to his mind. He only seeks to love God more, and the further he learns to tread in the way of perfection, the lighter he feels his yoke.

Cannot you see that it is mere folly to be afraid of giving yourself too entirely to God? It merely means that you are afraid of being too happy, of accepting His will in all things too heartily, of bearing your inevitable trials too bravely, of finding too much rest in His love, of letting go too easily the worldly passions which make you miserable. Try to despise all that is of the world that you may be wholly God's.

I do not say that you should cut yourself off from all earthly affections; to one who is leading a good, well-regulated life, all that is needed is that the motive power become that of love. You would then do very much the same things that you do now, for God does not usually alter the condition He has assigned to each or the duties appertaining thereto. The alteration would be that, whereas now you fulfill your duties for your own satisfaction and that of the world around, you would then pursue the same line as now. But instead of being eaten up by pride or passion — instead of living in bondage to the world's malicious criticism — you would act freely and bravely in the fullness of hope in God. You would be full of trust, and looking forward to eternal blessings would comfort you for the earthly happiness which seems to slip from under your feet. God's love would give wings to your feet in treading His paths and lifting you up beyond all your cares. If you doubt me, try: "O taste and see how gracious the Lord is!"

The Son of God says to all Christians without any exception, "If any man will come after Me, let him take up his cross and follow Me." (Matt. 16:24) The broad road leads to destruction; strive to follow that narrow path on which so few enter. Only the "violent take the Kingdom of Heaven by storm." You must be born anew, renounce and despise yourself, become as a little child, mourn that you may be comforted, and not be of this world, which is condemned because of unbelief.

These truths frighten many because they only see what religion requires without realizing what it offers, or the loving spirit by which it makes every burden light. They do not understand that such religion leads a person to the very highest perfection by filling him with a loving peace which lightens every woe. Those who have given themselves unreservedly to God are always happy. They realize that the yoke of Jesus Christ is light and easy, that in Him they do indeed find rest, and that He lightens the load of all that are weary and heavy laden, as He promised.

But what can be more wretched than those hesitating, cowardly souls which are divided between God and the world. They will and will not; they are torn asunder both by their own passions and by remorse at their indulgence; they are alike afraid of God's judgments and those of men; they are afraid of what is evil and ashamed of what is good; they have all the trials of goodness without its comfort! If they had but the courage to despise idle talk, petty ridicule, and the rash judgments of men, what peace and rest they might enjoy in the bosom of God!

Nothing is more perilous to your own salvation, more unworthy of God, or more hurtful to your ordinary happiness, than being content to abide as you are. Our whole life is given us with the object of going boldly on towards the heavenly home. The world slips away like a deceitful shadow, and eternity draws near. Why delay to push forward? While it is time, while your merciful Father lights up your path, make haste and seek His kingdom!

The first commandment of the law alone is enough to banish all excuse for any reserve with God: ''Thou shalt love the Lord thy God with all thy heart, and with all thy soul, and with all thy strength, and with all thy mind.'' (Luke 10:27) Observe how our Lord heaped together expressions which would forestall all the soul's evasions and reservations as regards God's jealous love, requiring not merely the heart's strength and power, but that of the mind and thought. Who can deceive himself by thinking he loves God if he does not willingly ponder His law, or try diligently to fulfill His holy will?

Be sure that all those who are reluctant to perceive fully what His love requires are yet a long way off from it. There is but one true way of loving God, *i.e.,* to do nothing save with and for Him, and to obey His call with a "free spirit." Those who aim at a compromise, who would like to hold onto the world with one hand, cannot believe this, and so they run the risk of being among those "lukewarm" whom God will reject. (Rev. 3:16)

Surely those cowardly souls which say, "Thus far will I go, but no farther," must be most displeasing to God. Is it fitting for the clay to dictate to the potter? What would men of the world think of a servant or a subject who presumed to offer such a half-service to his master or monarch, who shrank from a too hearty fulfillment of his duty, and was ashamed to let his loyalty be seen? And if so, what will the King of Kings say if we pursue such cowardly conduct? The time is at hand; He will soon come; let us prepare His way. Let us adore that eternal beauty which never grows old, and which imparts perpetual youth to such as love none else. Let us turn from this miserable world, which is already beginning to crumble away. How many great people we have seen pass away beneath the cold hand of death! We, too, shall soon be called to leave this world we love so dearly, and which is nought save vanity, weakness, and folly, — *a mere shadow passing away!*

26

On the Burden of Prosperity

Chains of gold are no less chains than those of iron. And while the wearer is an object of envy he or she is worthy of compassion. Your captivity is noways preferable to that of one kept unjustly in prison — the only real comfort is that it is God who deprives you of liberty, and this is the same comfort by which the innocent prisoner would be upheld. So all you have more than such an one is a phantom of glory, which gives you no real advantage, but exposes you to the risk of being dazzled and deceived.

But, after all, the consolation of knowing that you are where you are by God's providence is quite inexhaustible: while you have that, nothing can matter; and by it the iron chains are transformed, I will not say to gold — for we have just agreed that golden chains are nothing better! — but into liberty and happiness.

What is the good of that natural liberty of which we are so jealous? It only sets us free to follow our own unruly inclinations even in things lawful; to indulge pride and presume on independence; to carry out our own will, which is the very worst thing that can happen to us. Well it is for those whom God cuts off from their own will that they may follow His, and woe indeed to such as are bound by their passions; they are just as miserable as the others are blessed.

Those who are so bound cannot please themselves. From morning to night they do what God would have done, not what they like; so much the better! He holds them bound, so to say, hand and foot by His will. He never leaves them a moment to themselves. He is jealous of that tyrannous "I" which wants everything its own way. He leads them on from one sacrifice to another, from one trouble to another, and trains them to fulfil His noblest plans amid commonplace annoyances, frivolous society, and trivialities of which they feel ashamed. He urges the faithful soul till it has scarce time to draw breath: no sooner has one interruption ceased than God sends another to carry on His work. The soul would like to be free to think upon God, but all the while it is far more really united to Him by yielding to the cross He sends than by the most glowing, tender affections. He would like to be more his own in order to belong more to God! He forgets that one never so little belongs to God as when self asserts its claim. The "I" by means of which we fancy we can unite ourselves to God, puts a wider gulf between Him and us than the most ridiculous frivolity, for there is a venom in self which does not exist in mere childish amusement.

Of course you should make use of all available moments to loosen your bonds, and specially try to secure certain hours for the refreshment of body and mind by recollection; but as to the rest of the day, if the stream carries you away in spite of yourself, you must yield without regret. You will learn to find God amid the stream of distractions, and that all the more readily that it is not a self-chosen path.

Some He leads by bitter privations. Others He seems to lead by overwhelming them with the enjoyment of empty prosperity. He makes their lot hard and difficult by use of those very things which blind outsiders fancy to be the most perfect enjoyment of life! And so He carries on two good works in them — He teaches them by experience and causes them to die to self by the very things which foster evil and wickedness in many men. They are like that king we read of beneath whose hand turned to gold whatever he touched, and whose riches were his misery. But you can turn your worldly prosperity into a blessing by leaving everything to God, not even seeking to find Him except where and when He chooses to reveal Himself to you.

You must not wait for freedom and retirement to learn to let go. The prospect of such a time is very visionary — it may never come. We must all be ready, should it so please God, to die in harness. If He forestalls our plans for retirement, we are not our own, and He will only require of us that which it is in our power to give. The Israelites by the waters of Babylon longed sore after Jerusalem, yet how many were there not among them who never saw their own beloved country again, but ended their lives in Babylon! How great would their delusion have been had they postponed a hearty, true service of God until they could once more see their native land! Ah, well! It may be that our lot will be like those Israelites!

The discomfort you feel in this subject state is natural weariness craving for ease rather than any leading of God's Holy Spirit. You fancy you are missing God, but it is self you really miss; for the most trying side of this exciting life of constraint is that you are never free as regards *yourself*. It is the lingering spirit of self which would like a quieter state of things in which to enjoy its own intellect and gifts, and to air all its good qualities in the society of a chosen few who would soothe its self-consciousness; or, perhaps, it makes you wish to enjoy the consolations of religion in peace, just when God wills to send nothing but disturbance and contradiction, the more to mold you to His will.

27

On God's Various Crosses

God is very ingenious in making crosses for us. Some He makes of lead and iron, which are overwhelming in themselves; and some He makes of straw, which seem so light and yet are no less heavy to bear. Others he makes of gold and jewels, the glitter of which dazzles those around and excites the world's envy, but which all the while are as crucifying as the most despised of crosses.

He makes us crosses of whatever we love best, and turns all to bitterness. High position involves constraint and harassment; it gives things we do not care for, and takes away the things we crave.

The poor man who has not bread to eat finds a leaden cross in his poverty, and God mingles trouble very much akin to his with the cup of the prosperous. The rich man hungers for freedom and ease as the poor man hungers for bread; and whereas the latter can freely knock at every door and call upon every passer-by for pity, the man of high estate is ashamed to seek compassion or relief. God very often adds bodily weakness to this moral servitude among the great; and nothing can be more profitable than two such crosses combined: they crucify a man from head to foot, and teach him his own lack of power and the uselessness of all he possesses. The world does not see your cross — it only perceives some bondage softened by the possession of authority, and some slight indisposition which it probably attributes to fancy; while all the time you see nothing but bitterness, hardness, slavery, depression, pain, and impatience! All that dazzles the distant spectator vanishes before the eyes of its possessor, whom God nails to the cross, while all the world envies him or her.

So it is that Providence tries us in all manner of ways according to our position. Truly it is very possible to drink the cup of bitterness amid grandeur and without enduring calamity — nay to drink it to the very bitterest dregs out of the golden vessels which adorn the tables of kings! It is God's pleasure thus to confound human greatness, which is really no more than disguised powerlessness.

Happy are they who seek these things with that illumination of heart of which St. Paul speaks. Royal favor can give no real happiness; it can do nothing to remedy the most ordinary natural sufferings, while it adds many more, and those with sharp enough pangs, to what nature lays on us. The trials of high position are more acute than rheumatism or headache! But faith turns them all to good account: it teaches us to look upon all such things as a mere bondage, and in the patient acceptance thereof it shows us a real freedom, which is all the more real because it is hidden to our outward gaze.

No, the only good point of worldly prosperity is one to which the world is blind — its cross! An elevated position does not save us from any of the ordinary afflictions common to men; indeed, it has its own special trials, and furthermore, it involves a bondage which prevents people from seeking the relief open to those in a less exalted place. They who are not in a high place can at least, when ill, see whom they will, and be sheltered from outward disturbance; but the public person must carry his whole cross; he must live for others, when he fain would study his own comfort; he must put aside all wants, feelings, wishes, — must admit nothing to be an inconvenience, and must submit to all the restraints of his too good fortune. It is thus that God turns the good things which the world covets into trouble and toil — that He allows those whom He has raised to earthly grandeur to be an example to others. It is His will to perfect His cross by concealing it beneath the most splendid worldly prosperity, in order to show its little value.

Let me repeat, happy are those who in such circumstances learn to see God's hand bruising them in mercy. Surely it is a blessed thing to find one's "purgatory" in what seems a "paradise" to the worldly. In seeking that false paradise, many too often forfeit the hope of a true Paradise after this brief life ends.

The one real treasure of great seeming prosperity is its hidden Cross.

O Cross! Holy Cross! may I cleave to thee, may I worship my Lord as He hangs upon thee, and may I die with Him to sin and the world for ever! Amen.

28

On Simplicity and Self-Consciousness (I)

There is a simplicity which is merely a fault, and there is a simplicity which is a wonderful virtue. Sometimes it comes from a lack of discernment, and an ignorance of what is due others. In the world when people call anyone simple they generally mean a foolish, ignorant, credulous person. But real simplicity, so far from being foolish, is almost sublime. All good men like and admire it, are conscious of sinning against it, observe it in others, and know what it involves, and yet they could not precisely define it. One may apply to it what blessed Thomas à Kempis says in *The Imitation of Christ* about compunction of heart: "I would rather feel it than know how to define it." (Book I, Chapter I, 3)

I should say that simplicity is an uprightness of soul which prevents self-consciousness. It is not the same as sincerity, which is a much humbler virtue. Many people are sincere who are not simple — they say nothing but what they believe to be true, and do not aim at appearing anything but what they are; but they are continually in fear of passing for something they are not; and so they are for ever thinking about themselves, weighing their every word and thought, and dwelling upon themselves, in apprehension of having done too much or too little. These people are sincere, but they are not simple; they are not at their ease with others, or others with them; there is nothing easy, frank, unrestrained, or natural about them: one feels one would like less admirable people better, who were not so stiff! This is how men feel, and God's judgment is the same. He does not like souls which are self-absorbed, and always, so to say, looking at themselves in a mirror.

To be absorbed in the world around, and never turn a thought within, as is the blind condition of some who are carried away by what is present and tangible, is one extreme as opposed to simplicity. And to be self-absorbed in every-thing, whether it be duty to God or man, is the other extreme which makes a man wise in his own conceits — reserved, self-conscious, uneasy at the least thing which disturbs his inward self-complacency. Such false wisdom, in spite of its solemnity, is hardly less vain and foolish than the folly of those who plunge headlong into worldly pleasure. The one is intoxicated by his outer surroundings, the other by what he believes himself to be doing inwardly; but both are in a state of intoxication, and the last is a worse state than the first, because it seems to be wise, though it is not really, and so people do not try to be cured. They rather pride themselves on it, and feel exalted above others by it. It is a sickness somewhat like insanity — a man may be at death's door while affirming himself to be well.

He who is so carried away by outer things that he never looks within is in a state of worldly intoxication; and he who dissects himself continually becomes affected, and is equally far from being simple.

90

29

On Simplicity and Self-Consciousness (II)

Real simplicity lies in a happy medium, equally free from thoughtlessness and affectation, in which the soul is not overwhelmed by external things so as to be able to look within, nor yet given up to the endless introspection which self-consciousness induces. That soul which looks where it is going, without losing time arguing over every step, or looking back perpetually, possesses true simplicity.

The first step, then, is for the soul to put away things and look within as to know its own real interests. So far all is right and natural; thus much is only a wise "self-love" which seeks to avoid the intoxication of the world.

In the next step the soul must add the contemplation of God, whom it fears, to that of self. This is a faint approach to real wisdom, but the soul is still greatly self-absorbed; it is not satisfied with fearing God. It wants to be certain that it does fear Him, and fears lest it fear Him not, going round in a perpetual circle of self-consciousness. All this restless dwelling in self is very far from the peace and freedom of real love; but that is yet in the distance — the soul must needs go through a season of trial, and were it suddenly plunged into a state of rest, it would not know how to use it.

The first man fell through self-indulgence, and his descendants have to go through much the same course, gradually coming from out of self to seek God. For a while, then, it is well to let the penitent soul struggle with itself and its faults, before attaining the freedom of the children of God. But when God begins to open the heart to something higher and purer, then it is time to follow on the workings of His power step by step; and so the soul attains true simplicity.

The third step is that, ceasing from a restless self-contemplation, the soul begins to dwell upon God instead, and by degrees forgets itself in Him. It becomes full of Him and ceases to feed upon itself. Such a soul is not blinded to its own faults or indifferent to its own errors; it is more conscious of them than ever, and increased light shows them in plainer form. But this self-knowledge comes from God, and therefore it is not restless or uneasy.

Much anxious contemplation of our own faults hinders the soul as a traveler is hindered by an excessive quantity of bulky wraps, which prevent his walking freely. Superstition and scruples, and even, contrary as it seems at first sight, *presumption* grow readily out of such self-consuming processes. Real Christian simplicity is generous and upright, and forgets itself in unreserved resignation to God. If we men expect our earthly friends to be free and open-hearted with us, how much more will God, our best Friend, require a single-hearted, open, unreserved intercourse? Such simplicity is the perfection of God's true children, the object at which we should all aim. The greatest hindrance to its attainment is the false wisdom of the world which fears to trust anything to God — which wants to achieve everything by its own skill, to settle everything its own way, and indulge in ceaseless self-admiration. This is the wisdom of the world which St. Paul tells us is foolishness with God (I Cor. 3:19); whereas true wisdom, which lies in yielding one's self up unreservedly to God's Holy Spirit, is mere foolishness in the eyes of the world.

In the first stages of conversion we are forced continually to urge wisdom upon the Christian. When he is thoroughly converted, we have to fear lest he be "wise" overmuch, and it is needful to warn him that he "think soberly," as St. Paul says (Rom. 12:3); and when at last he craves a nearer approach to God, he must needs lose himself, to find himself again in God; he must lay aside that worldly wisdom which is so great a stay to self-reliant natures; he must drain the bitter cup of the "foolishness of the Cross," which has so often been the substitute for martyrdom with those who are not called on to shed their blood like the primitive Christians. When once all self-seeking and brooding is overcome, the soul acquires indescribable peace and freedom; — we may write about it, but only experience can really teach anyone what it is. The person who attains it is like a child at its mother's breast, free from fears or longings, ready to be turned hither and thither, indifferent as to what others may think, save so far as charity always would shun scandal; always doing everything as well as possible, cheerfully, heartily, but regardless of success or failure. Such a person embodies St. Paul's words: "It is a very small thing that I should be judged of man's judgment, yea, I judge not mine own self." (I Cor. 4:3)

On Simplicity and Self-Consciousness (III)

How far most of us are from real simplicity of heart! Still the farther we are the more urgently we should seek it. Yet so far from being simple, the greater number of Christians are not even sincere. They are not merely artificial, but often false and dissimulating towards their neighbors, towards God, and towards themselves. What endless little maneuvers and unrealities and inventions people employ to distort truth! Alas, "all men are liars!" Even those who are naturally upright and sincere, whose temper is what we call frank and simple, are often jealously self-conscious and foster a pride destroying all real simplicity which consists in genuine self-renunciation and forgetfulness of self.

How can you help being constantly self-engrossed when a crowd of anxious thoughts disturb you and set you ill at ease?

Do only what is in your own power to do! Never voluntarily give way to these disturbing anxieties. If you are steadfast in resisting them whenever you become conscious of their existence, by degrees you will get free. But do not hunt them out with the notion of conquering them! Do not seek a collision — you will only feed the evil. A continual attempt to repress thoughts of self and self-interest is practically continual self-consciousness, which will only distract you from the duties incumbent on you and deprive you of the sense of God's presence.

The great thing is to resign all your interest, pleasures, comfort, and fame to God. He who unreservedly accepts whatever God may give him in this world — humiliation, trouble, and trial from within or without — has made a great step towards self-victory. He will not dread praise or censure. He will not be sensitive. Or, if he finds himself wincing, he will deal so roughly with his own sensitiveness that it will soon die away. Such full resignation and unfeigned acquiescence is true liberty, and hence arises perfect simplicity. The soul which knows no self-seeking, no interested ends, is thoroughly candid; it goes on straight forward without any hindrance, its path opens daily more and more to "perfect day," and its peace, amid whatever troubles beset it, will be as boundless as the depths of the sea. But the soul which still seeks self is constrained, hesitating, smothered by the risings of self-love. Blessed indeed are they who are no longer their own, but have given themselves wholly to God.

The world takes the same view as God in this respect of a noble self-forgetting simplicity. The world knows how to appreciate among its own worldlings the easy, simple manners of unselfishness, and that because there is really nothing more beautiful and attractive than a thorough absence of self-consciousness. But this is out of keeping among worldly people, who rarely forget self unless it be when they are altogether absorbed by still more worthless external interests; yet even such simplicity of heart as the world can produce gives us some faint idea of the beauty of the real thing. They who cannot find the substance sometimes run after the shadow, and shadow though it be, it attracts them for want of better things.

Take a person full of faults, but not seeking to hide them, not attempting to sin, affecting neither talent, goodness, nor grace, not seeming to think more of himself than of others, not continually remembering that "I" to which we are most of us so alive: such a person will be generally liked in spite of many faults. His spurious simplicity passes as genuine. On the contrary, a very clever person, full of acquired virtues and external gifts, will always be jarring, disagreeable, and repulsive if he seems living in perpetual self-consciousness and affectation. So that we may safely say, that even from the lower point of view nothing is more attractive or desirable than a simple character free from self-consciousness.

But you will say, am I never to think of myself, or of what affects me? Am I never to speak of myself? No indeed, I would not have you so constrained; such an attempt at being simple would destroy all simplicity. What is to be done, then? Make no rules at all, but try to avoid all affectation. When you are disposed to talk about yourself from self-consciousness, thwart the itching desire by quietly turning your attention to God, or to some duty He sets before you.

Remember, simplicity is free from false shame and mock modesty, as well as from ostentation and self-conceit. When you feel inclined to talk about yourself from vanity, the only thing to be done is to stop short as soon as may be; but if, on the other hand, there is some real reason for doing so, then do not perplex yourself with arguments, but go straight to the point.

"But what will people think of me?" do you say? "I shall seem to be boasting foolishly, to be putting myself forward!"

All such anxious thoughts are not worthy of a moment's attention; learn to speak frankly and simply of yourself as of others when it is necessary, just as St. Paul often speaks of himself in his Epistles. He alludes to his birth, his Roman citizenship; he says that he was "not a whit behind the chiefest Apostles"; that he had done even more than they all; that he "withstood Peter to the face because he was to be blamed"; and that he had "been caught up into Paradise, and heard unspeakable words"; that he had "always a conscience void of offence toward God and toward men"; that he "labored more abundantly than they all"; he bids the faithful, "Be ye followers of me, even as I also am of Christ." See with what dignity and simplicity he always speaks of himself, and is able to say even the loftiest things without displaying any emotion of self-consciousness. He describes what concerns himself just as he would describe something that had happened a thousand years ago. I do not mean that we can or ought all to do the same, but what I do mean is that whenever it is right to speak concerning one's self, it should be done simply. Of course, every one cannot attain to St. Paul's sublime simplicity, and it were dangerous indeed to affect it; but when there is any real call to speak about yourself in ordinary life, try to do so in all straightforwardness, neither yielding to mock modesty nor to the shamefacedness which belongs to false pride, for indeed false pride often lurks behind a seemingly modest, reserved manner. We don't want to show off our own good points exactly; but we are very glad to let others find them out, so as to get double credit both for our virtues and our modesty in concealing them.

If you want to know how far you are really called upon to think or speak of yourself, consult someone who knows you thoroughly; by so doing, you will avoid self-opinionated decisions, which it is always a great thing to do. A wise spiritual guide will be much more impartial than we can ever be towards ourselves in judging how far we are justified in bringing forward our own good deeds; and as for unforeseen occasions rising up suddenly, all you can do is to look to God for immediate guidance, and do unhesitatingly what He seems to indicate. You must act promptly, and even should you be wrong, He will accept your right intention if you have sought with a single heart to do what you believed to be right in His eyes.

As to speaking of one's self in condemnation, I can say little. If a person does so in real simplicity, through a sense of abhorrence and contempt inspired by God, the results have been very marvellous among saints. But ordinarily for us who are not saints, the safest course is never to speak of one's self, either good or bad, needlessly. Self-love would rather find fault with itself than abide silent and ignored. As to your faults, you should be watchful to correct them. There are many ways of doing this, but as a rule, nothing is more helpful in the attempt than a spirit of recollection, a habit of checking eager longings and impulses, and entire resignation of yourself into God's hand without a constant fretting self-inspection. When God undertakes the work, and we do not frustrate Him, it goes on apace.

Such simplicity as this influences all things, outward manner included, and makes people natural and unaffected. You get accustomed to act in a straightforward way, which is incomprehensible to those who are always self-occupied and artificial. Then even your faults will turn to good, humbling without depressing you. When God intends to make use of you for His glory, either He will take away your failings or overrule them to His own ends, or at all events, so order things that they should not be a stumbling-block to those among whom He sends you. And practically, those who attain such real inward simplicity generally acquire with it an ingenuous, natural outward manner, which may even sometimes appear somewhat too easy and careless, but which will be characterized by a truthful, gentle, innocent, cheerful and calm simplicity, which is exceedingly attractive.

Verily such simplicity is a great treasure! How shall we attain it? I would give all I possess for it; it is the costly pearl of Holy Scripture. (Matt. 13:46) But the carnal mind is enmity against God, and "they that are after the flesh do mind the things of the flesh; and they that are after the Spirit, the things of the Spirit." (Rom. 8:5)

31

Rules for a Busy Life

You greatly need certain free hours to be given to recollection. Try to steal some such, and be sure that such little parings of time will be your best treasures. Above all, try to save your mornings; defend them like a besieged city! Make vigorous sallies upon all intruders, clear out the trenches, and then shut yourself up within your keep! Even the afternoon is too long a period to let go by without taking a breath.

Recollection is the only cure for your haughtiness, the sharpness of your contemptuous criticism, the sallies of your imagination, your impatience with inferiors, your love of pleasure, and all your other faults. It is an excellent remedy, but it needs frequent repetition. You are like a good watch which needs constant winding. Resume the books which moved you; they will do so again, and with greater profit than the first time. Bear with yourself, avoiding both self-deception and discouragement. This is a medium rarely attained; people either look complacently on themselves and their good intentions, or they despair utterly. Expect nothing of yourself, but all things of God. Knowledge of our own hopeless, incorrigible weakness, with unreserved confidence in God's power, are the true foundations of all spiritual life. If you have not much time at your own disposal, do not fail to make good use of every moment you have. It does not need long hours to love God, to renew the consciousness of His presence, to lift up the heart to Him or worship Him, to offer Him all we do or bear. This is the true Kingdom of God within us, which nothing can disturb.

32

God's Crosses Safer than Self-Chosen Crosses

The crosses which we make for ourselves by over-anxiety as to the future are not the Heaven-sent crosses. We tempt God by our false wisdom, seeking to forestall His arrangements, and struggling to supplement His providence by our own provisions. The fruit of our wisdom is always bitter. God allows it to be so that we may be frustrated when we forsake His Fatherly guidance. The future is not ours: we may never have a future; or, if it comes, it may be wholly different to all we foresaw. Let us shut our eyes to that which God hides from us in the hidden depths of His wisdom. Let us worship without seeing; let us be silent and lie still.

The crosses actually laid upon us always bring their own special grace and consequent comfort with them; we see the hand of God when it is laid upon us. But the crosses wrought by anxious foreboding are altogether beyond God's appointments. We meet them without the special grace adapted to the need — nay, rather in a faithless spirit, which renders grace impossible. And so everything seems hard and unendurable; all seems dark, helpless, and the soul which indulged in inquisitively tasting forbidden fruit finds nought save hopeless rebellion and death within.

All this comes of not trusting God, and prying into His hidden ways. "Sufficient unto the day is the evil thereof," our Lord has said, and the evil of each day becomes good if we leave it to God. What are we that we should ask Him, "Why doest Thou thus?" It is the Lord, and that is enough. It is the Lord: let Him do as seemeth Him good. Let Him lift up or cast down. Let Him wound or heal. Let Him smite or soothe. Let Him give life or death: He is always the Lord. We are but His work, a very toy in His hand. What matter, so long as He is glorified, and His will is fulfilled in us? Let us throw self aside, and then God's will, unfolding hour by hour, will satisfy us as to all He does in or around us. The contradictions of men, their inconstancy, their very injustice will be seen to be the results of God's wisdom, justice, and unfailing goodness. We shall see nothing but that infinitely good God, hidden behind the weakness of blind, sinful men.

The greatest of men are nothing of themselves, but God is great in them. He uses their caprices, their pride, their pretensions, vanity, and other wild passions, to set forward His everlasting purposes for His elect. He turns all within and without, the sins of others, our own failings, to our sanctification. All in Heaven and earth is designed to purify and make us worthy of Him. So let us be glad when our Heavenly Father tries us with various inward and outward temptations; when He surrounds us with external adversities and internal sorrows, let us rejoice, for thus our faith is tried as gold in the fire. It is this crucial experience which snatches us from self and the world. Let us rejoice, for by such travail the new man is born in us.

In the trials of life we learn the hollowness and falseness of all that is not God — hollowness, because there is nothing real where the one sole Good is not present; and falseness, because the world promises, kindles hopes, but gives nothing but emptiness and sorrow of heart — above all in high places!

Unreality must be unreal everywhere, but in high places it is all the worse because it is more decorated; it excites desires, kindles hope, and can never fill the heart. That which is itself empty cannot fill another. The weak, wretched idols of earth cannot impart a strength or happiness which they do not possess themselves. Do men seek to draw water from a dry well? Surely not. Then why should they look for peace and joy from great people who are ever complaining, who themselves cannot find amusement, and who are consumed with inward weariness amid all their outward display? ''They that make them are like unto them,'' as the Psalmist says of idolaters. (Ps. 115:8) Let us fix our hopes higher, further from the casualties of this life.

All that is not God will be found to be vanity and falsehood, and consequently we find both of these in ourselves. What is so vain as our own heart? With what delusions do we not deceive ourselves? Happy is he who is thoroughly undeceived, but our heart is as vain and false as the outer world; we must not despise that without despising ourselves. We are even worse than the world, because we have received greater things from God. Let us endure patiently, if the world fails or misuses us, as we have so often failed or misused God, grieving His Spirit of grace. The more the world disgusts us, the more it is furthering God's work, and while seeking to harm us, it will help us.

May you daily grow in these truths, that they may take deep root in your heart, and specially help you to be renewed in the Spirit of Jesus Christ.

"May the peace of God, which passeth all understanding, keep your heart and mind in Christ Jesus." Cut away every root of bitterness, and cast aside whatever disturbs the simple peace and trust of a child of God. Turn to your Father in every care; bury yourself in that tender Bosom, where nothing can fail you. Rejoice in hope, and casting aside the world and the flesh, taste the pure joys of the Holy Spirit.

May your faith be unmoved amid every storm, and may you ever remember the words of the great Apostle, "All things work together for good to them that love God, to them who are called according to His purpose." (Rom. 8:28)

33

On Lukewarmness

As to your lukewarmness and lack of conscious inward life, I am not surprised at this trial depressing you. Nothing is harder to bear. But it seems to me you have only two things to do, one of which is to avoid whatever excites and dissipates you. In this way you can cut off the source of dangerous distractions, which dry up prayer.

You cannot expect to find interior nourishment if you live only for what is exterior. Strict watchfulness in giving up whatever makes you too eager and impetuous in conversation is an absolute necessity if you would win the spirit of recollection and prayer. No one can have a relish for both God and the world simultaneously, and whatever spirit you have carried about with you through the day's occupations you will carry to the appointed hours of prayer.

Then, after cutting down whatever excesses distract your mind, you must try very often to renew the Presence of God, even amid those occupations which are right and necessary, guarding against your self-will. Try continually to act by the leadings of grace and in the spirit of self-renunciation. By degrees you will come to it, by frequently checking the impulsiveness of your lively disposition, and hearkening to God's voice within, letting Him possess you wholly.

34

On the Use of Seasons of Spiritual Peace

I am very glad that God gives you so much inward as well as outward peace. I pray that He who has begun this good work in you may fulfill it to the day of the coming of Christ. What you need now is to make use of these peaceful days to grow in recollection. You ought to sing with your whole heart the *Amen* and *Alleluia* which re-echo in the Heavenly Jerusalem. This is a token of continual acceptance of God's will, and the unreserved sacrifice of yours to His.

At the same time you should hearken inwardly to God, with a heart free from all flattering prejudices of self-love, so that you may faithfully receive His light as to the smallest of trifles which need correction. As soon as He points these out, we must yield without argument or excuse, and give up whatever touches the jealous love of the Bridegroom without reserve.

Those who yield in this manner to the Spirit of grace will see imperfection in their purest deeds, and an inexhaustible fund of refined evil in their hearts. All this leads them in self-abhorrence to cry out that God alone is good! They strive to correct themselves calmly and simply, but continuously, steadfastly, and that all the more because their heart is undivided and peaceful. They reckon on nothing as of themselves, and hope only in God. They give way neither to self-delusion nor laxity. They know that God never fails us, though we so often fail Him. They yield themselves wholly to grace, and above all things dread any resistance to it. They blame themselves without being discouraged. They bear with themselves while striving to amend.

35

On the Dangers of Intellectual Attractions

Do not trust too much in your intellect in your obedience. Do not obey a man because he can argue more forcibly or speak more feelingly than others, but because he is providentially ordered for you and is your natural superior, or because apart from all else you feel that he more than others is able to help you conquer your infirmities and attain to self-renunciation. A director is of little use in teaching detachment from self (death to self!) when it is self-will which seeks him.

Would that I could teach you true poverty of spirit! Remember what St. Paul says, "We are fools for Christ's sake, but ye are wise." (I Cor. 4:10) I would like to see in you no wisdom but that of grace, which leads faithful souls in the sure way when they do not yield to temper, to passions or self-will, or to any merely natural impulse. To such faithful souls, all that the world calls talent, taste, and good reasoning is as nothing.

Let me repeat: Beware of your own intellectual gifts and those of others; judge no one according to them. God, the only wise Judge, goes on a very different line. He gives preference to children and the childlike mind. Read nothing out of mere curiosity or in order to confirm your own opinions. Rather read with a view to foster a hearty spirit of meekness and submission.

Be as frank as a child towards those who counsel you. Make no count at all of your enlightenments or your extraordinary graces. Abide in simple faith, content to be obscure and unremitting in obedience to God's commandments. Act up to whatever God may make known to you through others, and accept meekly whatever may seem strange to you. Self-forgetfulness should take the shape of crushing out self-will, not of neglecting that watchfulness which is essential to the real love of God.

The greater your love, the more jealously you will watch over yourself, so that nothing may creep in unworthy of that love. May the Lord give you deeper understanding of these things than anything I can say, and Himself be all in all to you.

36

On the Use of Time

There is a wide difference between the mind's conviction and the right disposition of the heart, taking shape in diligent, dutiful practice.

Nothing has been commoner at all times, or now, than to meet with souls who are most perfect and saintly in what they believe, but "ye shall know them by their fruits," the Savior of the world has said. This is the only sure rule, if it be fairly dealt with — by this we must judge ourselves.

Time bears a very different aspect at different seasons of one's life, but there is one maxim which applies equally to all seasons: that none should go by uselessly; that all time forms a part of the order, a link in the chain of God's providence. Every season carries with it various duties of God's own appointing, and we must give account of how we have done them to Him, since from the first to the last moment of life, God never means us to look upon any time as purposeless.

The important thing is to know how He would have us use it. And this is to be learnt, not by restless, fidgety eagerness, which is more likely to confuse than enlighten us, but by hearty submission to those God has set over us, and by a pure, upright heart, simply seeking God, and by being diligent in resisting the deceits and wiles of self-love as quickly as they are recognized. For remember, we lose time not only by doing nothing, or doing amiss, but also by doing things in themselves right which yet are not what God would have us do. We are strangely ingenious in perpetual self-seeking; and the things which worldly people do overtly, those who want to serve God sometimes do with more refinement, under some pretext which hides the faultiness of their conduct.

One general rule for the right use of time is to accustom yourself to live in continual dependence upon God's Holy Spirit, receiving whatever He vouchsafes to give from one moment to another, referring all doubts to Him, and where an immediate course of action has to be taken, seeking strength in Him — lifting up your heart to Him whenever you become aware that outward things are leading you away, or tending to forgetfulness or separation from God.

Blessed is that soul which by sincere self-renunciation abides always in its Creator's hands, ready to do whatever He will, not weary of saying a hundred times daily, "Lord, what wilt Thou have me to do? Teach me to do Thy will, for Thou art my God. Send forth Thy light, Lord, to guide me; teach me to use the present time to Thy service. Forgive the misuse of what is past, and may I never blindly reckon on an uncertain future."

With respect to business and external duties, we need only to give a straightforward diligent heed to the ordering of God's providence. As all such duties are the result of His plans, we

114

have but to accept them dutifully, submitting our own tempers, fancies, inclinations, our self-will, perfectionism, our restless anxieties, our hurry — in short, all our own natural impulses to do what we like or how we like. Take care not to let yourself be overwhelmed by outer things, nor utterly immersed in external interests, however important.

Every undertaking should be begun with a definite view to God's glory, continued quietly, and ended without excitement or impatience.

Time spent in society and amusement is generally that most dangerous to one's self, though it may be very useful to others. Be on your guard, that is to say, be more faithful in remembering the Presence of God at such times. You need then especially to cultivate the watchfulness so often enjoined by our Lord — to use aspirations and liftings up of your heart to Him, as the only Source of strength and safety; otherwise you can scarcely hope to be kept from the subtle venom so often lurking amid society and its pleasures, or to be really useful to others. This is more than ever necessary for those whose position carries great weight, and whose words may do so much good or so much harm.

Spare time is often the pleasantest and the most useful as concerns one's self. It can hardly find a better use than of renewing our strength (and this bodily as well as mentally) through secret communion with God. Prayer is so necessary, it is the source of so much blessing, that when once the soul has realized its gifts, it will hardly fail to see them anew and so often as it is free to do so.

37

On the Loving Severity of God

Strict as God seems to you in His dealings with you, He never inflicts any suffering solely to give pain. He always has the purification of the soul in view. The severity of the operation is caused by the depth of the malady to be cured; God would not cut if there were no sore. He only probes the ulcerated proud flesh. So, after all, it is our own noxious self-will which is the cause of what we suffer, and God's hand deals as gently with us as may be. But how deep, how malignant our souls must be, since all the time He is sparing us so tenderly, yet He puts us to such grievous pain!

Again, just as God only wounds for our healing, so He never deprives us of any of His gifts, except to restore them a hundredfold. In His love, He takes away even His purest gifts if we are using them amiss; and the purer those gifts the more jealous He is that we should not reckon upon them as our own, or take credit to ourselves for them. The most notable graces turn to deadly poison if we rest upon them in self-complacent security. This was the sin of the fallen angels; so soon as they looked upon their exalted state as their own assured possession they became the enemies of God, and were driven forth from His Kingdom.

We may learn from this how little men understand about the real nature of sin. This is the greatest of all sins, yet there are but few souls so pure as to enjoy God's gifts without any intermixture of selfish complacency. In thinking of God's graces, self is almost always uppermost: we are troubled when we realize our own weakness. We take delight in conscious strength. We seldom weigh our own perfection solely with a view to God's glory, as we might do that of another person. We are saddened and depressed when the sensible sweetness and conscious grace forsake us. In short, we are almost always thinking not of God, but of self. And so all our good things need purifying, lest they foster a merely natural life in us. Our corrupt nature finds a very subtle food in the graces which are most opposed to nature; self-love is fed, not merely by humiliations and austerities, by fervent prayer and mortification — but even by the fullest self-renunciation and utter sacrifice. There is an infinite amount of moral strength in the thought that we have no strength at all, and that amid such a horrible trial we are still yielding ourselves up unreservedly. And so, to make the sacrifice real, we need that it too be consumed on the altar — we must give up even our satisfaction in that sacrifice!

The only way to find God truly is in this readiness to part with all His gifts, this thorough sacrifice of self, and of all inward resource. God's exceeding jealousy exacts it, and you can easily see how we never lose ourselves in Him until all else fails us. A man who is falling into an abyss is not wholly cast down so long as he can clutch hold of the sides. And self-love, even when God overthrows it, clutches in its despair at every gleam of hope, like a drowning man grasping at straws.

You must learn to realize the necessity of this deprivation of all God's gifts, which He gradually works out. There is no one gift, however precious, which, after having been a help, will not become a snare and a hindrance to the soul which rests in it; and so God often takes away that which He has given; not, however, wholly. He often deprives us of something only in order to restore it more fully, and without the evil spirit of self-satisfaction which had unconsciously got possession of us. This is overthrown by the loss, and then He restores it a hundredfold. And then the soul loses sight of the gift and sees God only.

38

Dryness and Deadness in Prayer

The soul, being diseased through self-love, cannot receive and rightly use a conscious strength. It is necessary therefore for God to conceal its strength, its growth, and good desires. Or, if it is permitted to see these, they must be seen as but a faint perception, so vague that the soul cannot rely on them; yet even so, it is prone to view such gifts with vain self-complacency, in spite of the humiliating uncertainty.

What would it not do if it were really able to behold clearly the grace which fills it? Therefore it is that God does two things for the soul, while He does but one for the body. To the body, He gives nourishment, together with the hunger and pleasure in eating, all of which are sensible. To the soul, however, He gives the hunger of desire, and food; but while giving these gifts, He hides them, lest the soul derive self-complacency through them. And thus, when purifying us with trial, He deprives us of delight, of sensible fervor, of acute conscious desires. As the soul in its pride turned all sensible power to poison, God reduces it to feel nothing but dullness, distaste, weakness, temptation. Notwithstanding these feelings, the soul does always receive real help; it is warmed, kindled, upheld in perseverance — but without the conscious enjoyment of all this, which is a very different thing from the fact. Prayer is not at all the same thing as the conscious pleasure which often is its accompaniment.

St. Teresa observes that many souls give up prayer as soon as they cease to find sensible pleasure in it, whereas this is to give up prayer just when it is on the way to be perfected. True prayer is not a matter of sense or imagination, but of the mind and will. But one may easily make mistakes in speaking of pleasure and delight. There is a pleasure altogether vague and indeliberate, which does not proceed from the will; and there is a deliberate pleasure, which is neither more nor less than a steadfast will. And this delight which comes of the deliberate will is that of which the Psalmist says, "Delight thou in the Lord, and He shall give thee thy heart's desire." (Psalm 37:4) This delight is inseparable from all real prayer, because it is in itself prayer; but this which is of the will is not always accompanied by that other delight, which is involuntary and sensible. The former may be most real, and yet not give any sensible consolation; and thus sometimes souls most severely tried may retain the delight of the will in an utterly dry prayer without conscious pleasure. Otherwise we should be reduced to saying that souls are only perfected in God's ways in proportion as they feel their pleasure in virtue increasing, and that all souls deprived of conscious pleasure by trial have lost the love of God, and are under delusion.

This would be to upset everything, and measure all piety by

the imagination, a proceeding which would tend to the most dangerous fanaticism, everyone deciding his own degree of perfection by the degree of his pleasure and taste. Moreover, this is really done by some souls consciously; they seek nothing save pleasure and satisfaction in prayer, and give themselves up to feeling, believing nothing to be real but what they feel and imagine — becoming mere enthusiasts. If they have a fit of fervor, they will enter upon and deal with anything; nothing stops them, no authority can restrain them. But if this sensible fervor dies out, forthwith such souls are disheartened, grow slack and fall away. They must be perpetually beginning again; they turn like a weathercock with every wind. They only follow Jesus Christ for the miraculous loaves and fishes. They demand quails in the desert; they are forever crying out like St. Peter on Mt. Tabor, "It is good for us to be here!" Happy the soul which is faithful alike in sensible abundance and in the most severe privation. It shall be "even as Mt. Zion, which cannot be removed, but stands fast forever." (Psalm 125:1)

Such a soul eats the daily bread of pure faith, neither seeking the enjoyment of anything which God denies it, nor the sight of anything He conceals. It is content to believe what the Church has taught it, to love God with a simple will; and to do, at all costs, whatever the Gospel commands or counsels. If satisfaction (in prayer and communion with God) is given, it accepts it as a help to its own weakness; if not, it bears the privation quietly, and loves on.

Clinging to what is sensible leads at one time to discouragement, at another to illusion. He who loses his sensible enjoyment of spiritual things without any fault of his own only suffers as a child when his mother weans him. Dry bread is less pleasant, but more strengthening than milk. A tutor's correction is more profitable than the fondling of a nurse.

We may be sure that we never need to pray so earnestly as when we cannot lay hold of any pleasure in prayer. That is the season of proving and trial, and consequently the time for most earnest recourse to God in urgent prayer. On the other hand, it is well to accept all feeling of devotion very simply, as given to feed, comfort, and strengthen the soul, never counting on such sweetness, for in such feelings the imagination often has its share in flattering us. Let us follow Jesus to His cross like St. John. In so doing we shall never be deceived. It is easy to say to oneself, "I love God with all my heart," when conscious of nothing but pleasure in such love. But true love is that which suffers while loving: "Though he slay me, yet will I trust him!" (Job 13:15)

39

On Peace of Conscience

There is never any peace for those who resist God. If there is any happiness in this world, it belongs to those whose conscience is pure. The whole earth is but pain and anguish to the evil conscience.

How different God's peace is from that which the world assumes, but cannot really give! God's peace quiets all passion and ensures purity of conscience. It unites a man to God, and strengthens him against temptation. This purity of conscience is preserved by frequenting the sacrament. All temptation, when resisted, bears its fruit for good; peace of heart lies in perfect acceptance of God's will.

"Martha, Martha, thou art careful and troubled about many things; but one thing is needful." (Luke 10:41,42) True simplicity, that calmness which results from complete submission to whatever God wills, patience and forbearance towards the faults of others, frankness in confessing your faults, accepting reproof, and receiving counsel — these are the solid graces which will serve as means toward your sanctification.

Anxiety comes from not sufficiently accepting whatever happens as coming from God. From the moment you give up all self-will, and seek absolutely nothing but what He wills, you will be free from all your restless anxiety and forecasting. There will be nothing to conceal, nothing to bring about. Short of that you will be uneasy, changeable, easily put out, dissatisfied with yourself and with others, full of reserve and mistrust. Your talents, unless chastened and humbled, will but torment you; your piety, though sincere, will do more in the way of inward reproach than of support and consolation. But once give yourself up to God, and you will be at rest, and filled with the joys of His Holy Spirit.

Woe to you if you lean upon man instead of God! In the matter of selecting a spiritual guide you must set aside all personal interests. The smallest degree of human respect will cut off grace, and increase your confusion. You will suffer greatly, and displease God.

We are constrained to love God because He first loved us, and that with a tender love, as a Father who pities His children, knowing their frailty, and the clay out of which He has formed them. He sought us in our own paths, which are sin. He followed us as a shepherd wearies himself in seeking his lost sheep. He is not content with finding us. Having found us, He carries us and our weariness — "He was obedient unto the death upon the Cross." "He loved us unto death" — and His obedience can only be measured by His love.

When a soul is filled with that love, it will enjoy peace of conscience, and be content and happy. It will need neither grandeur, fame, pleasure, nor anything which passes away; it will crave nothing but the will of God, but will watch continually in a blessed expectation of the Bridegroom's coming.

40

On Slackness

I can find no words better suited to you than those of St. John to the Church at Ephesus: "But I have this against you, that you have abandoned the love you had at first. Remember then from what you have fallen; repent and do the works you did at first. If not, I will come to you and remove your lampstand from its place, unless you repent." (Rev. 2:4,5) It is thus that God's Holy Spirit loves men without flattering them. He loves, yet threatens, but His very threats are love. He holds forth a penalty, so that men may not force Him to inflict it.

See how easily the best people fall gradually away without noticing it. Here is Timothy (supposed to be Bishop of Ephesus) whom St. Paul addresses as a "man of God" (I Tim. 6:11), the angel of one of the holiest churches in the East in those days of religious prosperity; yet this angel falls; he "leaves his first love," his recollection, his prayer, his good works; he grows lax and careless. At first he does not perceive his wanderings or his fall. He says to himself, "What harm am I doing? Is not my conduct upright and regular in the world's eyes? Must one not have some pleasure? It is scarce worth living without anything to cheer and amuse one!" It is thus that people cleverly deceive themselves, and disguise their backsliding. But the Holy Spirit bids them hasten to open their eyes, and see "from whence they are fallen."

How far are you below your former standard! Remember the fervency of your prayers, your love of solitude, your jealous watch over your quiet time, and the strictness with which you shunned whatever could interfere with it. If you do not remember, others have not forgotten, and do not fail to ask, "What has become of all that fervor? There is nothing to be seen now but the love of amusement and pleasure, and a restless inward boredom when there is a pause in these. It is not the same person."

Thus unaware, people fall by degrees and under plausible pretenses go from a state of sincere self-denial into a laxity which revives all the worst forms of selfishness. You should try to "remember whence you are fallen," and mourn over that "first love" which fostered you. You must try to resume those "first works" which you have exchanged in such a slothful way for mere vanities. You must gaze from afar on the desert in which you dwelt at peace with the true Comforter. You must say with the prodigal son, "I will arise and go to my Father, and will say unto Him, 'Father, I have sinned against Heaven and against Thee, and am no more worthy to be called Thy son.' " If you fail in returning speedily to His Fatherly breast, you heard what He would do: "I will come to you, and will remove your lampstand from its place." He would take away the light which you do not use, and leave you in darkness. He would transfer His precious gifts which you have trodden underfoot to some truer, more obedient soul. You must resume your reading, your prayers, your silence, your former simplicity and lowliness.

41

On Openness and Candor

Nothing is more useful than speaking out freely. Open your heart; we heal our woes by not hugging them. We learn simplicity and yieldedness, for people are only reserved about things which they do not mean to give up. Finally, we humble ourselves, for nothing is more humbling than to open one's heart and lay bare all one's weaknesses, yet nothing draws down a greater blessing.

I do not mean that you should always tell all you may be thinking with scrupulous exactness. This would be endless, and you would be forever uneasy for fear of having forgotten something. Simply keep back nothing out of untruthfulness or false shame of self-love, which would never willingly show anything but its fair side. If you never thus intend to keep back anything, you may safely say less or more, as seems best for the occasion.

It is not a question of feelings, but of the will. Often our feeling does not depend at all upon ourselves. God takes it away purposely that we may feel our poverty, that we may learn to accept the cross of inner dryness, and that we may undergo the purification of clinging to Him without any sensible consolation, and then He restores to us the comfort of warm feelings from time to time out of pity for our weakness.

Try to take an attitude towards God, not of forced conversation such as you maintain with persons towards whom you stand on ceremony and address in a mere complimentary fashion, but such as you observe towards a dear friend with whom you are under no restraint, and who is under none with you. Such friends meet and talk and listen, or are silent, content to be together saying nothing; — their two hearts rest in one another; — they are but as one; they do not weigh what they shall say; they insinuate nothing, have no hidden agenda — all comes forth in truth and love, regardless of arrangement; nothing is held back or perverted or dressed up. They are just as well satisfied one day when a little has been said as another when there was plenty to say.

We can never be as real with our best earthly friends as fully as we could wish, but we can be so to any extent with God, if only we will not hedge ourselves in with our own self-love. It will not do to pay Him visits, as we discharge a debt due to society. We must abide with Him in the privacy of servants, or better still, of children. Be with Him as you would have your child be with you, and then you will never be weary.

42

On Patience
Under Contradiction

A heated imagination, vehement feeling, a world of argument, and a flow of words, are really useless. The practical thing is to act in a spirit of detachment, doing what one can by God's light, and being content with such success as He gives.

Such continuous death to self is a blessed life which but few realize. A single word quietly spoken under such influences will go further, even in worldly matters, than the most eager, bustling exertions. It is the Spirit of God, speaking with His own strength and authority. He enlightens, persuades, touches, edifies. Scarcely anything has been said, but everything has been done.

On the contrary, when people let loose their natural excitability, they talk interminably, indulge in endless, subtle, superfluous imaginations. They are afraid of not saying or doing enough. They get warm and excited; they exhaust themselves without anything being the better for it.

Let the river flow beneath its bridges. Let men be men, that is to say, weak, vain, inconstant, unjust, false, presumptuous. Let the world be the world, in short; you cannot hinder it. Let everybody follow their natural disposition and habits; you cannot remold them. It is easier to let them alone and bear with them. Accustom yourself to put up with unreasonableness and injustice.

Abide tranquilly in God's bosom. He sees all these evils more clearly than you do, yet He suffers them. Be content with doing well what little depends upon you, and let all else be as though it were not.

I must warn the reader to keep such advice in perspective. This is not counsel to irresponsible passivity, but to letting go the urge to control, or to uselessly fret over what we cannot change. —Ed.

43

On Bearing Affronts

You greatly need God's Holy Spirit to guide you in your
difficulties, and to moderate your natural vehemence
under circumstances so calculated to excite it.

As to those who have caused this difficulty, I think you
should speak of that to none save to God in prayer on behalf
of the person who insulted you. I have often fancied you to
be very sensitive on that point, and God always touches us in
our weak place. Men are not killed by a blow on the extremi-
ties — the nails or the hair — but by an injury to the vital
parts. When God purposes to make us die to self, He always
touches that which is the very essence of our life. He adapts
our cross to each one of us.

Let yourself be humbled; calm and silence under humiliation are a great benefit to the soul. One is sometimes tempted
to talk about humility, and it is easy to find plenty of opportun-

ities for so doing, but it is better to be humbly silent. Talkative humility is always suspicious; talk is a certain relief to self-conceit.

Do not get angry about what people say. Let them talk while you try to do God's will. As to the will of men, you could never come to an end of satisfying it, nor is it worth the trouble. Silence, peace, and union with God ought to comfort you under whatever men may falsely say. You must be friendly to them, without counting on their friendship. They come and go. Let them go — they are but as chaff scattered by the wind.

Only see God's hand in what they do. He wounds or comforts us through their means. You need all your resolution, but at the same time your quickness of temper requires checks and impediments. Possess your soul in patience.

Frequently recall the Presence of God, so as to calm yourself, to humble and adapt yourself to the humble of heart. Nothing is really great save lowliness, charity, mistrust of self, detachment from one's own opinions and will. All stiff, harsh goodness is contrary to Jesus Christ.

44

On Freedom from Self

So long as we are centered in self, we shall be prey to the contradiction, the wickedness, and the injustice of men. Our temper brings us into collision with other tempers; our passions clash with those of our neighbors; our wishes are so many tender places open to the shafts of those around; our pride, which is incompatible with our neighbors', rises like the waves of a stormy sea; — everything rouses, attacks, rebuffs us. We are exposed on all sides by reason of the sensitiveness of passion and the jealousy of pride.

No peace is to be looked for within when we are at the mercy of a mass of greedy, insatiable longings, and when we can never satisfy that "me" which is so keen and touchy as to whatever concerns it. Hence in our dealings with others we are like a bed-ridden invalid who cannot be touched anywhere without pain. A sickly self-love cannot be touched without screaming; the mere tip of a finger seems to scarify it! Then add to this the roughness of neighbors in their ignorance of self, their disgust at our infirmities (at the least as great as ours towards theirs), and you soon find all the children of Adam tormenting each other, each embittering the other's life.

And this martyrdom of self-love you will find in every nation, every town, every community, every family, often between friends.

The only remedy is to renounce self. If we set aside, lose sight of, self, we shall have nothing to lose, to fear, or to consider. Then we shall find that true peace which is given to "men of good will," that is, those who have no will save God's, which has become theirs.

Then men will not be able to harm us. They can no longer attack us through hopes or fears, for we shall be ready for everything, and refuse nothing. And this is to be inaccessible, invulnerable to the enemy. Man can only do what God permits, and whatever God permits him to do against us becomes our will, because it is God's. So doing, we shall store our treasure so high that no human hand can reach to assail it. Our good name may be tarnished, but we consent, knowing that if God humbles us, it is good to be humbled. Friendship fails us: well! it is because the one true Friend is jealous of all others, and sees fit to loosen our ties. We may be worried, inconvenienced, distressed; but it is God, and that is enough. We love the Hand which smites; there is peace beneath all our woes, a blessed peace.

We desire nothing which is denied us; and the more absolute this self-renunciation, the deeper our peace. Any lingering wishes and clingings disturb it. If every bond were broken, our freedom would be boundless. Let contempt, pain, death, overwhelm me, still I hear Jesus Christ saying, "Fear not them which kill the body but are not able to kill the soul.'' (Matt. 10:28) Powerless indeed are they; even though they can destroy life, their day is soon over! They can but break the earthen vessel, kill that which voluntarily dies daily. Anticipate somewhat the welcome deliverance, and then the soul will escape from their hands into the bosom of God, where all is unchanging peace and rest.

45

On the Presence of God

The real mainspring of all perfection you will find contained in the precept given of old by God to Abraham: "Walk before Me, and be blameless." (Gen. 17:1) The presence of God will calm your spirit, — it will give you peaceful nights, and tranquillize your mind even amid the hardest day's work; but then for this you must give yourself up unreservedly to God. When once you have found God, you will realize that you need not seek anything more among men; you must be ready to sacrifice even your dearest friendships, for the best of friends is the indweller of hearts. He is as a jealous bridegroom, who will tolerate no rival near him.

You do not need much time to love God, to renew the thought of His presence frequently, to lift up your heart to Him and worship Him in its depths, to offer Him all you do and all you suffer; and this is the real "Kingdom of God within you," (Luke 17:21) which nothing can disturb.

If outward distractions and your own lively imagination hinder your soul from conscious recollection, in any case you must practice it in your will; so doing the desire for recollectedness will become in itself a kind of recollection which will avail, especially if you turn resolutely towards God and to whatever He requires of you with a steadfast intention.

Try at intervals to kindle within yourself a hearty desire to give yourself to God to the fullest extent of all your powers; your mind to know and think upon Him, and your will to love Him; and endeavor also to consecrate all your outward actions to Him. Be on your guard not to let yourself be engrossed too entirely, or for any length of time, with anything external or interior, the tendency of which is so to distract your heart and mind as to make it difficult for you to turn fully towards God.

The moment you feel that any outside object causes you too much pleasure or delight, sever your heart from it, and lest you should stop short in the creature, turn yourself at once to your only true End and sovereign Good, God Himself. If you are steadfast in breaking off all creature-worship, and in reserving to God alone that love and reverence which He requires, you will soon experience that true happiness which He never fails to give to the soul which sits loosely to all earthly affections. When you are conscious that you are longing very earnestly for anything whatsoever, or that you are too keenly excited about anything in which you are engaged, be it great or small, try to pause, and remember that God Himself tells us His Holy Spirit is not to be found in the storm or the whirlwind. Be watchful not to throw yourself too actively into all that is going on, nor let yourself become too engrossed by it; for this is one great source of distractions.

As soon as you have ascertained what the Lord would have you to do in each matter as it arises, stop there, and give no heed to all the rest. So doing you will be able to keep your mind calm and composed, and to shake off an infinity of useless matters which hamper the soul and hinder it from turning fully to God.

One excellent method of maintaining inward calmness and freedom is to keep putting aside all useless reflections on the past, whether of regret or self-complacency, and when one duty is accomplished, to go steadily on with the next, — confining your attention entirely to the one thing God gives you to do, and not forestalling difficulties for the future any more than regrets for the past. Again, accustom yourself to make a frequent brief act of God's presence through the day, and amid all your occupations; whenever you are conscious that anxiety or disturbance are springing up within, calm yourself in this way: cut yourself off from all that is not of God; cut short useless thoughts and broodings; avoid unprofitable talk. If you seek for God within your heart, you will infallibly find Him, and with Him peace and happiness.

As to your active occupations, try even in those to let God have the largest share. If you would fulfil your commonest duties well, you must do them as in His presence and for His sake. The sight of His majesty and love will calm and strengthen you. A word from the Lord stilled the raging of the sea (Mark 6), and a glance from us to Him, and from Him to us, will do the same in our daily life.

Lift up your heart continually to God; He will purify, enlighten, and direct it. Try to be able to say with the holy King David, "I have set God always before me," (Ps. 16:9) and again: "Whom have I in heaven but Thee, and there is nothing on earth that I desire besides Thee . . . . Thou art the strength of my heart, and my portion for ever." (Ps. 73: 24,25) Do not wait till you can be alone to seek a recollected mind; the moment you become conscious of having lost recollection, strive to renew it.

Turn to God simply, familiarly, trustfully. This can be done even amid the greatest interruptions as well as not, even when you are wearied and pestered with uncongenial society. All things, be sure, "work together for good to those that love God." (Rom. 8:28)

You must be regular with such spiritual reading as is suited to your needs, making frequent pauses to hearken to the Voice which will help to call your inner self to recollection. A very few words thus studied are a true manna to the soul. You may forget the actual words, but they are taking root all the time secretly, and your soul will feed upon them and be strengthened.

46

On Seeing Ourselves in God's Light

Forgetfulness of self does not interfere with gratitude for His gifts. And for this reason: such forgetfulness does not lie in being unmindful of anything we possess, but rather in never confining ourselves to the contemplation of self, or dwelling upon our own good or evil in an exclusive or personal fashion. All such self-occupation severs us from pure and simple love, narrows the heart, and sets us further from true perfection by reason of seeking it in an excited, anxious, restless spirit, which comes of self-love.

But though we may forget ourselves, that is to say, we may not be studying self-interest alone, we shall not fail often to see ourselves truly. We shall not contemplate self out of egotism, but as we contemplate God there will often be a side light, so to say, thrown upon ourselves; just as a man who stands looking at the reflection of another in a large mirror, while looking for that other man he beholds himself, without seeking to do so. And thus we often see ourselves clearly, in the pure light of God. The presence of God in purity and simplicity, sought after in very faithfulness, is like that large mirror, wherein we discern the tiniest spot that flecks our soul.

A peasant who has never passed beyond his own poor village only faintly realizes its poverty. But set him amid splendid palaces and courts, and he will perceive how squalid his own home is, how pathetic his rags, compared with such magnificence. Even so we realize our own loathsomeness and unworthiness when brought face to face with the beauty and greatness of God.

Talk as much as you will of the vanity and emptiness of the creature, the shortness and uncertainty of life, the inconstancy of fortune and friends, the delusions of grandeur, its inevitable and bitter disappointments, the failure of bright hopes, the vanity of all we attain, and the pain of the evils we endure. All these things, true and fair as they are, do not touch the heart, they do not reach far, or alter a man's life. He sighs over the bondage of vanity, yet does not seek to break his bonds.

But let one ray of heavenly light penetrate within, and forthwith beholding the depth of goodness, which is God, he likewise beholds the depth of evil, His fallen creature. Then he despises himself, hates, shuns, fears, renounces self; he throws himself upon God and is lost in Him. Thus it is that "one deep telleth another." Verily that man's loss is a blessed one, for he finds himself without seeking. He has no more selfish interests, but all turns to his profit, for everything turns to good to those who love God.

He sees the mercies which flow into his weakness, sin, and nothingness; he sees and rejoices. And here observe that those who have not as yet made any great progress in self-renunciation still see all these mercies very much in relation to their personal interests. For thorough setting aside of self-will is so rare in this life, that very few souls are able to look at the mercies they have received from anything but their own point of view. They rejoice in the all-powerful hand which has saved them, so to say, in spite of themselves.

But a really pure, wholly self-detached soul, such as are the saints in heaven, would feel the same joy and love over the mercies poured forth on others as on themselves. For, wholly forgetting self, they would love the good pleasure of God, the riches of His grace, and His glory, as set forth in the sanctification of others, as much as in their own. All would be the same, because "I" ceased to be: it would be no more "I" than another, but God alone in all, to be loved, adored, and the sole joy of true, disinterested love. Such a soul is rapt in wonder at His mercies, not for its own sake, but for love of Him. It thanks Him that He has done His will and glorified Himself, even as in the Lord's Prayer we ask Him that it may be done, and that His kingdom may come . . . .

But short of this blessed state, the soul is touched with gratitude for the benefits of which it is conscious. And as nothing is more dangerous than any attempt to soar beyond our vocation, so nothing is more harmful to the spiritual life than to lose sight of such sustenance as is suitable to its actual needs, by aiming at a higher standard of perfection than is fitted to us. When the soul feels deeply moved with gratitude for all God has done for it, such gratitude should be cherished carefully, waiting till the time when God may see fit to purify it still more from all elements of self.

The child who attempts to walk alone before its time is sure to fall; he must not tear off the leading-strings with which his nurse upholds him. Let us be content to live on gratitude, and be sure that though there may be a mingling of self-interest in it, it will strengthen our heart. Let us love God's mercies, not merely for Himself and His glory, but for ourselves and our eternal happiness. If eventually God should enlarge our hearts to contain a purer, more generous love, a love more unreservedly His, then we may safely and unhesitatingly yield to that more perfect love.

While, then, you adore God's mercy, and are filled with wondering admiration at it; while you long above all things to fulfil His will; while you marvel at the goodness with which He has made what seemed a "vessel of dishonor" to be unto honor (Rom. 9:21), pour out the most abundant thanksgiving of which you are capable. And remember that the purest of all God's gifts is the power to love them all for His sake, not for your own.

47

On the Privation of
Sensible Sweetness

It is long since anything has pleased me more than your letter of yesterday . . . . You must accustom yourself to privation: the great trouble it causes shows how much it is needed. It is only because we appropriate light, sweetness, and enjoyment, that it is so necessary that we should be stripped of all these things. So long as the soul clings to any consolation, it needs to be stripped thereof. Undoubtedly the God we feel to be beneficent and indulgent is still God, but it is God with His gifts: God surrounded with darkness, privation, and desolation is God only. When a mother wants to attract her little one, she comes to him, her hands full of toys and sugarplums; but the father approaches his grown-up son without any presents. God goes still further; He veils His face, He hides His presence, and often only visits those He seeks to perfect through the utter darkness of simple faith.

You are like a baby crying because you have missed your bonbons. God gives them to you now and then, and these ups and downs comfort the soul when it begins to be discouraged, while accustoming it at the same time to privation.

God does not intend either to spoil or discourage you. Give yourself up then to these changes which so upset your soul. By accustoming it to having no abiding condition, they make it supple and plastic to receive whatever impression God wills. It is God's way of melting and molding your heart so that all the outlines of self are lost. Pure water has neither color nor form; it always takes the form and color of the vessel containing it. Let this be your case with God.

As to painful or humiliating thoughts, whether concerning your faults or your temporal affairs, treat them as the sensitiveness of self-love. Our pain at all these things is more humiliating than the things themselves. Put all together, the trouble and your perplexity at it, and carry the cross without trying to alter it one way or another. As soon as you bear it in this way, in simple trust of God, you will be at rest, and your cross will become light.

48

On Conformity to the Will of God (I)

You will find several chapters in the *Imitation* on Conformity to God's Will, which are marvelous, and also a great deal more helpful in St. Francis de Sales. The whole gist of the matter lies in the will, and this is what our dear Lord meant by saying, "The Kingdom of God is within you." (Luke 27:21) It is not a question of how much we know, how clever we are, nor even how good; it all depends upon the heart's love. External actions are the results of love, the fruit it bears; but the source, the root, is in the deep of the heart. Some virtues are suitable to one condition in life, some to another; some to one season, some to another. But at all seasons and in all places we need a will that is good.

That kingdom of God within us consists in always willing whatever God wills, wholly, unreservedly. It is thus that our prayer "Thy Kingdom come" is fulfilled; thus that "His will is done in earth as in heaven"; thus we become, so to say, identified with Him. Blessed are the poor in spirit! Blessed are they who strip themselves of all they can call their own, even their will; for this it is to be truly poor in spirit.

But how, you ask, are you to acquire this saintly will? By absolute conformity to that of God; by willing what He wills and desiring nothing which He does not will; by nailing, so to say, your feeble will to His all-powerful will. If you do this, nothing can happen which you do not will, nor can anything happen save that which God orders; and you will find unfailing comfort and rest in submitting to His will and pleasure. Such a life within is indeed a foretaste of the blessedness of the saints, and their everlasting song, Amen, Alleluia!

As you learn to worship, praise, and bless God for all things, — to see His hand everywhere, — you will feel nothing to be an unbearable evil; for everything, even the most cruel sufferings, will "turn to good" for you. Who would call *evil* the sorrows which God lays on him with a view to purify and make him fit for Himself? Surely what works out such exceeding good cannot be evil? Cast all your cares into the bosom of your loving Father. Let Him do as He sees fit with you. Be content to obey His will in all things, and to merge your will concerning everything in His. What right have you, who are not your own, to any intrinsic possession? A slave has no proprietary rights; how much less the creature which in itself is mere sin and nothingness, and which can possess nought save by the gift of God? God has endowed it with freewill in order that it may have something real to offer Him. We have nothing to call our own save our will, — nothing else is ours. Sickness takes away health and life; riches melt away; mental powers depend upon a man's bodily strength; — the one and only thing really ours is our will. And consequently, it is of this that God is jealous, for He gave it, not that we should use it as our own, but that we might restore it to Him, wholly and undividedly. Whoever holds back any particle of reluctance or desire as his right defrauds his Maker, to whom all is due.

49

On Conformity to the Will of God (II)

A las! how many self-asserting souls we meet, — people who would like to do right and love God, but only after their own fashion and choice, — who practically lay down the law to God as to His dealings with them! They wish to serve Him and possess Him and let Him possess them. And as a natural result, how much resistance God meets with from such people, even when they seem full of zeal and ardor for His service! To a certain degree, indeed, their spiritual abundance becomes a hindrance, because they look upon it as their own, and self-assertion mingles in their best works. Verily, the soul which is utterly impoverished, utterly devoid of self-existence, incapable of willing aught from hour to hour save that which God sets before it in the precepts of His gospel and the ordering of His providence, is far ahead of all those fervid enlightened people who persist in travelling to heaven by their own self-chosen path.

This is the real meaning of those words of Jesus Christ: "If any man will come after me, let him deny himself, and take up his cross, and follow me." (Matt. 16:24) We must *follow* Him step by step, not strike out a new road of our own, by "denying" self. And what is it to deny self but to renounce all rights over self? Even as St. Paul says: "Ye are not your own." (I Cor. 6:19) Woe to those who take back the gift when once it is made.

Pray to the Father of mercies, the God of consolation, that He would tear out all that is of self in you, leaving no remnant behind. So painful an operation must be hard to bear. It is very difficult to lie still under God's hand while He cuts to the quick; but this is the patience of saints, the offering of pure faith. Let God do as He will with you. Never resist Him voluntarily even for a moment. The instant you become conscious of the revulsion of nature and inclination, turn trustfully to Him; take His side against your own rebellious nature; give it up to God's Holy Spirit, and ask Him to put it by degrees to death. Watch, as in His sight, over your most trifling faults; strive never to grieve the Holy Spirit, who is so jealous over your hidden life. Make use of past faults to attain a humble consciousness of your own weakness, only without weariness or discouragement.

How could you give more glory to God than by absolutely setting aside self and all its longings, and letting Him send you where He pleases? It is thus that He will be your God, that His kingdom will come in you, if independently of all outward hindrances and helps you look to nothing, within or without, save God's hand overruling all things, your own unfailing worship.

If you persist in serving Him in one place or one way rather than another, you are serving Him according to your will, not His. But if you are ready to go anywhere and do anything, if you leave yourself to be entirely molded by His providence, putting no limits to your submission, this is indeed taking up your cross and following Him. Then you would be perfectly happy if He were to lay the heaviest trials on you for His great glory.

Open your heart wide, unboundedly wide, and let God's love flow in as a torrent. Fear nothing on your way. God will lead you by the hand, if only you trust Him wholly, and are filled rather with love for Him than fear for yourself.

50

On Seeking Help in Inner Trouble

I am not at all surprised at your trouble — it is natural you should feel it; only it should make you feel your helplessness, and lead you to have humble recourse to God. When you feel that your heart is sinking under trouble, be simple and frank in saying so. Do not be ashamed to let your weakness be seen, or to ask help in your urgent need. So doing you will advance in simplicity, in humility and trustfulness; you will go far to root out self-love, which keeps up a perpetual disguise in order to seem cheerful when it is really in despair. Furthermore, try to amuse yourself with whatever may lighten your solitude and keep off weariness or boredom without exciting or wearing yourself out with worldly pleasures. If you nurse your troubles in silence they will grow stronger and finally overpower you, and the unreal courage which self-love creates will cause you a world of harm. The poison which goes into the system is deadly; that which comes forth does no great mischief. You must not be ashamed of seeing a free discharge from the sore in your heart. I take no heed whatever of certain expressions which escape you, and which are merely the utterance of suffering in spite of your real self. It is enough if such expressions teach you that you are weak, and if you learn not to hide and cherish your weakness, but bring it to the light that it may be cured.

51

On Legalism and Freedom

It seems to me desirable that you should combine great exactitude with great liberty. The first will cause you to be faithful, the latter courageous. If you aim at being exact without freedom, you will fall into scruples and bondage. If, on the other hand, you affect freedom without exactness in duty, you will soon yield to negligence and laxity. Mere exactness in the fulfilment of duty narrows heart and mind; mere liberty stretches them too widely. They who have no experience in God's ways do not believe it possible to combine the two virtues. By being exact they understand living in a state of constraint and exhaustion, in a restless, scrupulous timidity which deprives the soul of all freedom. They look for sin lurking everywhere, and so narrow the soul's vision that it frets about every trifle and scarcely dares to breathe. By freedom they mean having a very lax conscience, ready to pass over detail; being content to avoid serious faults, and calling serious nothing save gross crimes; indulging freely in whatever is acceptable to self-love, and taking considerable license as to the passions, in the thought that they meant no great harm. This was not the freedom St. Paul contemplated when he wrote to his children in grace, whom he was trying to train up to Christian perfection: "Ye have been called unto liberty; only use not liberty for an occasion to the flesh." (Gal. 5:13)

It seems to me that real liberty consists in obeying God in all things, and in following the light which points out our duty, and the grace which guides us. We should take as our rule of life the intention to please God in all things; not only always to do what is acceptable to Him, but if possible what is *most* acceptable. It is good not to trifle with petty distinctions between great sins and small, imperfections and faults, — for although it may be very true that there are such distinctions, they should have no weight with a soul which is determined to refuse nothing it possesses to God. It is in this sense that the Apostle says, "The law is not made for a righteous man": (I Tim. 1:9) — a burdensome, hard, threatening law, one might almost say a tyrannical, enslaving law. But there is a higher law which rises above all this, and which leads him into the true "liberty of sons," — the law which makes him always strive to do that which is most pleasing to his Heavenly Father, in the spirit of those beautiful words of St. Augustine: "Love, and then do what you will."

Exactness and liberty ought to keep abreast, and if one halts with you rather than the other, I thing it is liberty. Although I freely confess that your exactitude has not yet reached the point I could desire. Still, on the whole, I believe that you need to put more emphasis on the side of confidence in God and enlargement of heart. Therefore I do not hesitate to say that you ought to yield wholly to the grace with which God sometimes draws you closer to Him. Do not be afraid to lose sight of self, to fix your gaze solely and as closely upon Him as He will permit, and to plunge wholly into the ocean of His love — happy if you could do it so entirely as never to come forth again. Nevertheless it is well, whenever God gives you such a happy disposition, to accept it with humility and with loving, childlike fear, so as to make ready for fresh gifts. This is the counsel St. Teresa gives, and I think it may safely be given to you.

52

On the Right Use of Crosses

The more we fear to bear Crosses, so much the more do we need them: let us not, therefore, fall in hopeless discouragement, when the hand of God lays them heavily upon us: we should rather judge of the magnitude of our disease by the severity of the remedies which our spiritual Physician sees good to apply. Truly must we be most diseased, and God most merciful, since, notwithstanding our opposition, He deigns to heal us: surely, we should find in our very crosses a fund of love, of consolation and confidence, saying with the Apostle, "Our light affliction, which is but for a moment, worketh for us a far more exceeding weight of glory." (II Cor. 4:17) Happy are they who weep, and who, having sown in tears, shall with ineffable joy reap the harvest of eternal life.

"I am crucified with Christ," says St. Paul (Gal. 2:20) It is with our Savior that we are bound to the Cross, and it is His grace which binds us there. It is for Jesus' sake that we would not quit the Cross, since without it we cannot have Him.

O adorable and suffering Body, in and with which we are forever united, give me, together with Thy Cross, Thy spirit of love and self-denial; teach me rather to think of the privilege of suffering with Thee, than of the pangs of that suffering. What can I suffer which Thou hast not endured? or rather, how dare I presume to speak of suffering, when I remember what Thou hast borne for me? O weak man, be silent; behold thy Master, and be silent! Lord, teach me to love Thee, and I shall fear no Cross. Then, come what may of grievous and bitter pangs, I shall never have more to bear than I am glad and willing to bear.